BILATERAL INVESTMENT TREATY CLAIMS

THE ESSENTIALS

Also by Khawar Qureshi in the *Wildy's Legal Handbook Series:*

Public International Law Before the English Courts ISBN: 9780854901951

Conflicts of Interest in International Arbitration: An Overview ISBN: 9780854901937

WILDY'S LEGAL HANDBOOK SERIES

BILATERAL INVESTMENT TREATY CLAIMS

THE ESSENTIALS

Khawar Qureshi QC

WS
&H

Wildy, Simmonds & Hill Publishing

Bilateral Investment Treaty Claims: The Essentials

ISBN 9780854901944

British Library Cataloguing in Publication Data

A catalogue record for this book is available from the British Library

First published in 2016 by

Wildy, Simmonds & Hill Publishing
58 Carey Street
London WC2A 2JF

MIX
Paper from
responsible sources
FSC
www.fsc.org   FSC® C013604

CONTENTS

FOREWORD   vii

INTRODUCTION   1

BACKGROUND   3

  ICSID Caseload statistics   3

  Research tools   4

KEY ISSUES   5

  What is a BIT?   5

  Contents of a typical BIT   5

BIT CLAIM CHECKLIST   9

  When did the BIT enter into force?   10

  Time of alleged breach?   10

  Is there an Investor?   11

  Is there an Investment?   15

  Fair and Equitable Treatment?   19

  Has there been expropriation of the investment? 26

  Breach of full protection and security   32

  Are there Most-Favoured Nation Provisions Implications?   33

  Are there "Umbrella Clauses"/Implications?   36

  Are there explicitly incorporated procedural requirements?   36

  Is there sufficient evidence to make out a prima facie
  case of breach of a BIT?   39

  Is there evidence of a "knock out" point such as the
  payment of a bribe?   40

What is the claim worth? What are "just and equitable" damages? 40

ADDITIONAL CONSIDERATIONS 48

Preliminary/provisional measures 48

Security for costs 56

Abuse of process 58

Illegality 62

Third party funding 62

ROLE OF NATIONAL COURTS 68

Supporting investment treaty arbitration proceedings 68

Enforcement of Investment Arbitration Awards 70

ANNEX 1: Sample Bilateral Investment Treaty 75

ANNEX 2: Relevant Legislation, Rules and Guidelines 115

(i) Extracts of ICSID Convention 115

(ii) ICSID Arbitration Rules 131

(iii) ICSID Enforcement Act (England and Wales) 166

(iv) Code of Conduct for Litigation Funders (January 2014) 170

ANNEX 3: Recent BIT Arbitration Decisions Which Impact Upon Key Concepts 177

FOREWORD

Bilateral investment treaties (BITs) have become the dominant feature of international investment law. So much so, that nowadays the two concepts are often used synonymously.

The significance of BITs is usually discussed in terms of their impact on investment streams and hence on economic development. A frequently overlooked aspect of BITs is their effect on international relations. Diplomatic protection by the investor's State of nationality, exercised on the basis of often ill-defined legal principles, used to be a frequent source of discord and irritation. By introducing legal rules into a hitherto largely unregulated area, BITs have depoliticized disputes and brought a measure of legal security into the field. In the presence of objective treaty standards, supported by an effective investor-State dispute settlement mechanism, the host State and the investor's home State are less likely to be drawn into investment disputes.

The multitude of bilateral treaties in the area of investment protection has created a confusing picture of patchwork regulation. Despite their large numbers, BITs by no means cover all foreign investments. Moreover, the diversity of standards and procedures offered by BITs has led to considerable inequality among investors of different nationalities in different countries. The appropriate remedy is often seen in the, as yet, unattainable goal of a grand multilateral treaty. But there are benefits to bilateralism and the resulting fragmentation. BITs offer a high degree of flexibility to States in deciding with whom and to what extent they wish to enter into treaty relations on investment protection. The diversity of economic relations among States and disparate ideas about the preferred modes of investment protection stand in the way of universally acceptable standards.

A comparative study of BITs displays similar features and recurrent standard clauses. But a closer look also reveals a surprising number of variations. Not all familiar features and standard clauses appear in all BITs. Not all recurrent features are exactly alike. Therefore, in practice, the application of these treaties requires careful scrutiny of each individual document.

The present volume is a most useful manual for practitioners and students alike. It offers a practice-oriented overview of the most important features of BITs and their application by tribunals.

Christoph Schreuer

Rudolf Dolzer

INTRODUCTION

The purpose of this text is to provide an overview of a rapidly growing area of litigation concerning Investor Protection – Bilateral Investment Treaty Disputes.

Many readers will already be familiar with BITs. The initial 4 chapters provide background to BITs and their key features, along with a checklist for practitioners contemplating or involved in a claim under a BIT.

The penultimate chapter covers additional considerations, as well as leading cases dealing with the scope for preliminary measures in Investment Treaty cases, abuse of process and illegality.

Annex 1 is an example of a BIT entered into between China and Canada which came into force on 1 October 2014.

Annex 2 is a non-exhaustive schedule of some recent BIT arbitration decisions which impact upon key concepts within BITs.

Once you have read a few BIT cases (unwieldy as they are) and represented clients in them, a familiar pattern emerges: filing of a claim, delay in appointing the Tribunal, a procedural order which is inevitably violated. Thereafter, a hearing on jurisdiction which mostly results in the Tribunal finding jurisdiction. After 4 years or so, if and when a Merits award is produced, the claim is very often dismissed or an award is made for a sum significantly less than sought.

Nevertheless, there are very real signs (in recent decisions) that arbitral tribunals are now recognising the need to produce expeditious, clear, coherent and consistent decisions. This is a very important and welcome development.

This text is current as at January 2016.

BACKGROUND

BIT disputes are a rapidly expanding and high profile area of international litigation. The World Investment Report 2015 (Reforming International Investment Governance) shows that there were 7 known BIT cases in total as at 1996. By 2012, the number was 514.

However, although rapidly expanding in numbers, Investment Treaty disputes still comprise less than 10% of the total number of international arbitrations.

Nevertheless, given the potential utility of BITs for foreign investors and the scope for claims against States, it is vital to be aware of the key features of Investment Treaties – whether from the perspective of advising on the negotiation of an inward investment agreement (and hence considering issues such as strategic use of jurisdictions which have Investment Treaty arrangements with the host state), or when considering a potential claim against a State.

ICSID Caseload statistics

ICSID publishes statistics relating to its caseload twice yearly. The following statistics are based on the most recent published caseload report (2015-2, current to November 2015).

New cases per annum:

- 2008: 21
- 2009: 25
- 2010: 26
- 2011: 38
- 2012: 50
- 2013: 40
- 2014: 38
- 2015 (up to 30 June 2015): 28

3

As of 30 June 2015, ICSID had registered 525 cases under the ICSID Convention and Additional Facility Rules.

Other key statistics include:

- 61% of ICSID cases are based on BITs for jurisdiction;

- 25% of cases concern South American State Parties and 25% concern Eastern Europe/Central Asia State Parties;

- 26% of cases are in the Oil, Gas and Mining sector. 15% are in the Electrical power and energy sector;

- 64% of cases lead to an award. 36% of proceedings are discontinued or settled;

- 75% of cases lead to an award on the merits. 25% of awards decline ICSID jurisdiction;

- 70% of arbitrators in ICSID cases are from North America and Western Europe;

- The top 3 nationalities for ICSID arbitrator appointments are French (181), United States (178) and British (148) (as at 30 June 2015).

Research tools

The following are helpful websites for those interested in further research:

- UNCTAD - research data on trends in BIT negotiations/ disputes and a very good database of BITs (www. unctad.org)

- ICSID - case list, procedural orders, decisions on jurisdiction/merits and BIT list (https://icsid.worldbank. org)

- ECT - case list, information relating to Energy Charter Treaty 1994 (www.energycharter.org)

KEY ISSUES

What is a BIT?

These are Treaty arrangements used to provide foreign investors with a "level playing field" and access to an international arbitral tribunal in the event that the host State uses its sovereign power with detrimental effect to the foreign investor.

The first BIT was entered into in 1959 (in the wake of the Cold War and nationalisations which exposed the lack of effective protection for foreign investors). By the end of 2008, there were almost 3,000 BITs. Many are linked to multilateral treaty-based systems such as the ICSID Convention (1965) and the Energy Charter Treaty (1994).

Contents of a typical BIT

Whilst it is vital that the specific treaty provisions engaged are always examined carefully, most BITs follow a similar approach vis-à-vis contents.

1. Preamble – limited legal effect (provides context for interpretation)

2. Definitions – the main ones being definitions of "Investor" and "Investment". There is an increasing tendency in new BITs for States to require commercial presence/substantial business activities for nationality qualification qua investor).

3. Scope of Protection – core provisions:

   - Fair and equitable treatment (including denial of justice) ("FET"),

   - Full protection and security,

   - Expropriation.

   - "Procedural (or substantive) bonuses"

- Most-Favoured Nation Provisions ("MFN") (depending on which ICSID decision you read, these permit an investor to "cut and paste" more favourable provisions from any other BIT which the Host State has entered into).

- "Umbrella clauses" (again depending on which ICSID case you read and the exact wording of the provision, these "elevate" a contractual obligation to the realm of Treaty obligation).

4. Procedure (General)

5. Other Incorporated Procedures

6. Jurisdictional provisions

- Settlement of disputes between the Host State and an investor

- Entry into force of the BIT

- Duration of the BIT

As BITs are treaties, the obligations undertaken by States are governed by Public International Law. There was very little development by way of International Law jurisprudence on key concepts such as the meaning of expropriation for decades, due to ideological differences as to the role of investors.

Hence, anyone coming to this area will find that most of the "learning" is recent (within the past 15 years) and essentially comes from decisions of international arbitral tribunals such as the ICSID Tribunal.

ICSID and ECT decisions are normally publicly available. There is a move to also make pleadings in these cases publicly available, along with (the recent development of) "amicus" briefs (see, for example, *Suez, Sociedad General de Aguas de Barcelona S.A. and Interagua Servicios Integrales de Agua S.A. v. Argentine Republic* (ICSID Case No. ARB/03/17) (Order in response to a Petition for Participation as Amicus Curiae, 19 May 2005). Two reasons may explain the stark contrast (vis-à-vis the apparent openness of the process) with most international arbitrations which are controlled by strict confidentiality requirements:

1. There is a perceived strong public interest in the "investor community" and citizens of a "Host State" being informed as to the existence and nature of investor disputes

2. There is a very real problem with regards to the lack of any system of precedent vis-à-vis arbitral decisions in this area. No doctrine of precedent exists, as per the Tribunal's remarks in *Abaclat v Argentina* (Decision on Jurisdiction, 4 August 2011): "*The Tribunal shares the generally accepted view that the decisions of ICSID tribunals, like those of other investment dispute settlement mechanisms, are not legally binding precedents. Consequently, the Tribunal does not consider itself bound by previous decisions of other international tribunals. However, the Tribunal is also of the opinion that, subject to the specific provisions of a treaty in question and of the circumstances of the actual case, it should pay due consideration to earlier decisions of international tribunals, where it believes that such consideration is appropriate in the light of the specific factual and legal reasoning of these earlier decisions*". Conflicting decisions are not uncommon (often reflecting the quality of the arbitrators and/or the desire of the tribunal to "push" a certain argument).

Many States that were hitherto blissfully ignorant as to the significance of BITs have been taken by surprise as to their meaning and effect. Indeed, there have been an increasing number of threats by States to seek re-negotiation of BITs and/or their termination.

On 2 May 2007, the World Bank received a written notice of denunciation of the ICSID Convention from the Republic of Bolivia. In accordance with Article 71 of the ICSID Convention, the denunciation takes effect six months after the receipt of Bolivia's notice (on 3 November 2007). Thereafter, Ecuador acted in a similar manner on 4 December 2007 and Venezeula on 25 January 2012, and other states have stated an intention to withdraw from the ICSID Convention.

Further, on 22 April 2013, seven Latin American countries (Bolivia, Cuba, the Dominican Republic, Ecuador, Nicaragua, Saint Vincent and the Grenadines, and Venezuela) adopted a declaration on "Latin American States affected by transnational interests", in which they agreed to establish an institutional framework to deal with challenges posed by transnational companies, especially legal claims brought against governments under BITs. The declaration also supported the creation of a regional arbitration centre to settle investment disputes and an international observatory for cooperation on international investment litigation.

BIT CLAIM CHECKLIST

How to spot a BIT claim: Is there a claim involving a State entity where it might be argued that an investment has been detrimentally affected by the use of State authority?

Assuming you have located an applicable BIT, when advising on a BIT matter, always ask the following questions to evaluate whether the BIT provisions are engaged, and the nature/extent of any potential claim thereunder:

1. When did the BIT enter into force (and is it still in force)?

2. Was the alleged BIT breach by the State after its entry into force or is it a continuing breach?

3. Is there an Investor?

4. Is there an Investment?

5. Has there been an absence of Fair and Equitable Treatment?

6. Has there been expropriation of the investment?

7. Are there Most-Favoured Nation Provisions ("MFN")/ Implications?

8. Are there "Umbrella Clauses"/Implications?

9. Are there explicitly incorporated procedural requirements?

10. Is there sufficient evidence to make out a prima facie case of a breach of the BIT?

11. Is there evidence of a "knock out" point such as the payment of a bribe?

12. What is the claim worth? What are "just and equitable" damages?

When did the BIT enter into force?

Typically, all BITs will contain an article which sets out when the provisions become effective.

However, even after a contracting state has terminated a BIT, that BIT may still apply for a certain length of time. See, for example, a typical clause which provides:

> *With respect to investments made prior to the date of termination of this Agreement, the provisions of Articles 1 to 15 shall continue to be effective for a further period of ten years from such date of termination.*

Time of alleged breach?

A BIT will typically contain a provision which states that the provisions will only apply to disputes that arise after the treaty comes into force:

> *This Agreement shall apply to investments, which are made prior to or after its entry into force by investors of either Contracting Party in the territory of the other Contracting Party in accordance with the laws and regulations of the other Contracting Party concerned in the territory of the latter, but shall not apply to a dispute that arose before the entry into force of this Agreement.*

Accordingly, it can be important to determine precisely when a dispute has arisen between the parties, particularly where there have been ongoing discussions.

In *Standard Chartered Bank (Hong Kong) Limited v. Tanzania Electric Supply Company Limited* (ICSID Case No. ARB/10/20) (Decision on Jurisdiction and Liability, 12 February 2014), the tribunal identified four jurisdictional requirements that must be met:

- first, a condition ratione personae: the dispute must concern a Contracting State and a national of another Contracting State;

- second, a condition ratione materiae: the dispute must be a legal dispute arising directly out of an investment;

- third, a condition ratione voluntatis, i.e. the Contracting State and the investor must consent in writing that the dispute be settled through ICSID arbitration;

- fourth, a condition ratione temporis: the ICSID Convention must have been applicable at the relevant time.

In *Ping An Life Insurance Company of China, Limited and Ping An Insurance (Group) Company of China, Limited v. Kingdom of Belgium* (ICSID Case No. ARB/12/29) (Award, 30 April 2015), the Tribunal (which declined jurisdiction over the dispute) considered in detail the interplay between successive BITs between two countries, and the implications and application of retroactivity.

BIT Claim Checklist

In *Lao Holdings N.V. v Lao People's Democratic Republic* (ICSID Case No. ARB(AF)/12/6) (Decision on Jurisdiction, 21 February 2014), the Tribunal rejected the argument that any party may at any time refer to arbitration "legal disputes" that were dealt with before the investor State's accession to the Treaty. In that case, nothing in the Treaty contemplated that investors such as the Claimant could change their nationalities at will by artful corporate restructurings to "forum shop" after a legal dispute has arisen with the same investor on the same issue. On that basis, it was important to ascertain when the dispute actually arose.

Is there an Investor?

There exists a very broad definition of investor – so long as a national of a BIT State party (natural or legal entity) can claim to have made an investment in the Host State party to the same BIT, the fact that a locally incorporated entity is used to conduct business is no bar to a BIT based claim.

For a time, the majority decision in *Waguih Elie George Siag and Clorinda Vecchi v. The Arab Republic of Egypt*, ICSID Case No.

ARB/05/15 (Decision on Jurisdiction, 11 April 2007) seemed to threaten significant potential for abuse. The Claimant was an Egyptian national at all material times when the investment was made, and then allegedly lost his Egyptian nationality, acquired Lebanese nationality and also Italian nationality – he claimed under an Italy/Egypt BIT. The majority held that the ICSID nationality requirement (Article 25 ICSID Convention) was satisfied and that the Claimant had lost Egyptian nationality, despite the fact that his acquisition of Lebanese/Italy nationality appeared to be a device. The minority view was that Egyptian nationality had not been lost and was the real and effective nationality (which meant that as a national of the Host State the Claimant's claim was barred).

Subsequent cases have somewhat allayed these fears. In *Pac Rim Cayman LLC v. The Republic of El Salvador* (ICSID Case No. ARB/09/12) (Decision on the Respondent's Jurisdictional Objections, 1 June 2012) it was held that the dividing line in determining whether a change of nationality can become an abuse of process occurs *"when the relevant party can see an actual dispute or can foresee a specific future dispute as a very high probability and not merely as a possible controversy [...].The answer in each case will, however, depend upon its particular facts and circumstances..."* (para. 2.99).

In that case the tribunal found that since the basis of the claim (El Salvador's de facto ban on mining in 2008) occurred after Pac Rim Cayman's change of nationality in 2007, the dispute could not have been foreseen by the claimant (para. 2.109).

In *Al Tamimi v Sultanate of Oman* (ICSID Case No. ARB/11/13) (3 November 2015), an ICSID Tribunal (comprising Professor David A R Williams QC as President, along with Judge Charles N Brower and Mr J Christopher Thomas QC) considered, inter alia, whether the alleged dual nationality (UAE and US) of the claimant prevented him from claiming as an investor under the Oman-US Free Trade Agreement. The Tribunal dismissed the Respondent's objection that the claimant held dual nationality – on the evidence, the Tribunal found that the claimant was a national only of the US. However, the Tribunal also held that even if the claimant had held dual nationality, and his "dominant and effective nationality" (as that term was defined in the FTA) was that of a third state, this would not have prevented him invoking the FTA. The Tribunal considered that the provision is aimed at preventing claims by dual nationals of both State parties (ie the United States and Oman) from seeking to use the FTA to claim against their own State of dominant and effective nationality – thereby defeating the purpose of the FTA to apply investment protection only to "investors of the other Party".

In *Standard Chartered Bank v. The United Republic of Tanzania* (ICSID Case No. ARB/10/12) (Award, 2 November 2012) it was further held that to get the benefit from Article 8(1)'s arbitration provision, a claimant must demonstrate:

1.   that the investment was made at the claimant's direction,

2.   that the claimant funded the investment or

3.   that the claimant controlled the investment in an active and direct manner (para 230).

An indirect chain of ownership linking the British claimant to debt owed by a Tanzanian borrower did not satisfy the requirement in the Treaty's arbitration provision. The tribunal reasoned that, despite the fact that the claimant owned a substantial equity interest in a Hong Kong company, which in turn held Tanzanian debt acquired from Malaysian financial institutions, it could not be said that those loans were the claimant's investments (paras. 196-197).

It should also be remembered that the ICSID Convention contains its own (undefined) requirement of Investor/ Investment (Article 25 ICSID Convention) which can sometimes act as a second hurdle vis local corporate entities where the issue of effective "investor" control is raised – see *Suez, Sociedad General de Aguas de Barcelona S.A. and Interagua Servicios Integrales de Agua S.A. v. Argentine Republic* (ICSID

Case No. ARB/03/17) (Decision on Jurisdiction, 16 May 2006) (at paragraphs 38 to 40 thereof).

The fact that the "foreign" investor (company) is 99% owned by nationals of the Host State, and that there is no evidence to show "inflow of capital" might appear to disqualify a party from claiming to be an "investor" – this is not necessarily the case (see the case of *Tokios Tokelés v. Ukraine*, ICSID Case No. ARB/02/18 (Decision on Jurisdiction, 29 April 2004) and the dissenting opinion of Professor Prosper Weil who contended that the "real investor" in this case was a Ukraine national and not a Lithuanian company, and that "investments made in a State by its own citizens with domestic capital through the channel of a foreign entity" did not fall within the object and purpose of BIT protection).

More recently, in *National Gas SAE v Arab Republic of Egypt*, ICSID Case No. ARB/11/7 (Decision, 3 April 2014), the Tribunal declined jurisdiction over a dispute. In doing so, the Tribunal considered the approach to be taken by tribunals considering the limits of ICSID jurisdiction and the requirements of the "foreign control" test in Article 25(2)(b) of the ICSID Convention. In that case, notwithstanding that Mr Ginena, an Egyptian-Canadian dual national, had chosen his corporate structure for legitimate fiscal reasons and not as an exercise in forum shopping, the corporations which owned the shares in the Claimant were mere shell companies masking the fact that Mr Ginena was the Claimant's true controller. Therefore, the Claimant was not under "foreign control" and the Tribunal did not have jurisdiction over the dispute.

Tribunals are increasingly alive to the issue of forum shopping, which has been addressed in a number of cases (discussed further in relation to abuse of process below).

KT Asia Investment Group B.V. v Republic of Kazakhstan (ICSID Case No. ARB/09/8) (Award, 17 October 2013) established that if a Claimant was an investor within the terms of the relevant BIT, which provided that a legal entity constituted under the laws of one country was an investor, without the need for any further requirements, then no further requirements (such as the need for real and effective control) could be added. In *Alps Finance and Trade AG v. The Slovak Republic*, UNCITRAL (Award, 5 March 2011), it was held that if a BIT imposes a requirement of having a seat and real economic activity in the host state, this requirement has the purpose of excluding "mailbox" or "paper" companies from its protection.

Is there an Investment?

Generally

Investment is often defined as "Every kind of asset" – a very broad concept.

BIT Claim Checklist

In the case of *Bayindir Insaat Turizm Ticaret Ve Sanayi A.S. v. Islamic Republic of Pakistan*, ICSID Case No. ARB/03/29 (Decision on Jurisdiction, 14 November 2005), the dispute provided a good opportunity for the Tribunal to rule on a very expansive challenge to knock out the claim on jurisdictional grounds. The claim against Pakistan had been brought by a Turkish contractor whose agreement to build a motorway in Pakistan had been affected (allegedly) by, inter alia, the imposition of additional taxes, favouritism to local contractors and corruption. The ICSID Tribunal rejected all of Pakistan's contentions. On the issue of the nature of an investment, the Tribunal stated (at paragraph 116) that it could not be *"seriously disputed that Bayindir's contribution in terms of know-how, equipment and personnel clearly has an economic value and falls within the meaning of "every kind of asset""*.

The case of *Caratube International Oil Company LLP v. The Republic of Kazakhstan* (ICSID Case No. ARB/08/12) (Award, 5 June 2012) held that "investment" was understood by the tribunal as *"an economic arrangement requiring a contribution to make profit, and thus involving some degree of risk"* (para. 455.) The tribunal found *"no plausible economic motive"* to explain the US national's investment in CIOC, no evidence of a contribution of any kind (the US national's personal guarantees for a loan received by the company from a Lebanese bank were not

15

considered as constituting a sufficient contribution in this case) or any risk undertaken by the US national, and no capital flow between the US national and CIOC (para. 455).

Under Article 25 of the ICSID Convention

A set of objective criteria was identified in the case of *Salini Costruttori S.p.A. and Italstrade S.p.A. v. Morocco* (Decision on Jurisdiction, 23 July 2009) – "*The doctrine generally considers that investment infers: contributions, a certain duration of performance of the contract and a participation in the risks of the transaction. In reading the Convention's preamble, one may add the contribution to the economic development of the host State of the investment as an additional condition*".

These criteria have been the subject of much discussion in later cases.

The criteria have been described as guidelines rather than "mandatory requirements", as set out in *Philip Morris Brand Sàrl (Switzerland), Philip Morris Products S.A. (Switzerland)* and *Abal Hermanos S.A. (Uruguay) v. Oriental Republic of Uruguay* (ICSID Case No. ARB/10/7) (Decision on Jurisdiction, 2 July 2013) – "*the four constitutive elements of the Salini list do not constitute jurisdictional requirements to the effect that the absence of one or the other of these elements would imply a lack of jurisdiction. They are typical features of investments under the ICSID Convention, not "a set of mandatory legal requirements". As such, they may assist in identifying or excluding in extreme cases the presence of an investment but they cannot defeat the broad and flexible concept of investment under the ICSID Convention to the extent it is not limited by the relevant treaty, as in the present case.*"

In *Electrabel S.A. v. Republic of Hungary* (ICSID Case No. ARB/07/19) (Decision on Jurisdiction, Applicable Law and Liability, 30 November 2012) it was held that, in relation to the criteria of investment, "*[w]hile there is incomplete unanimity between tribunals regarding the elements of an investment, there is a general consensus that the three objective criteria of a contribution, a certain duration, and an element of risk are necessary elements of* an investment." Moreover, economic development of the host State, whilst desirable, was "not necessarily an element of an investment" (para. 5.43).

The case of *Deutsche Bank AG v. Democratic Socialist Republic of Sri Lanka* (ICSID Case No. ARB/09/2) (Award, 31 October 2012) held that:

1. regularity of profit and return should not be used as additional benchmarks.

2. *"the existence of an investment must be assessed at its inception and not with hindsight"*(para. 295).

3. a contribution can take any form and it is not limited to financial terms but also includes know-how, equipment, personnel and services (para 297).

4. short-term projects are not deprived of "investment" status solely by virtue of their limited duration. Duration is to be analysed in light of all the circumstances and of the investor's overall commitment (paras 303-304).

In *Quiborax S.A., Non Metallic Minerals S.A. and Allan Fosk Kaplún v. Plurinational State of Bolivia* (ICSID Case No. ARB/06/2) (Decision on Jurisdiction, 27 September 2012), it was held that the following are not part of the normal definition of investment:

1. contribution to the development of the host State;

2. conformity with the laws of the host State; and

3. respect of good faith (para. 219).

A distinction was made *"between the objects of an investment, 'such as shares or concessions [...] and the action of investing'"*. While shares or other securities or title may be the legal materialization of an investment, mere ownership of a share is, in and of itself, insufficient to prove a contribution of money or assets (para 233).

This reasoning agreed with the decision in *Daimler Financial Services AG v. Argentine Republic* (ICSID Case No. ARB/05/1)

BIT Claim
Checklist

(Award, 22 August 2012) which held that ICSID claims were *"at least in principle separable from their underlying investments"* and thus the claimant's ICSID claims *"were [not] necessarily and automatically transferred along with the shares by operation of law."* (para. 145) Instead, any qualifying investor who suffered damages as a result of the governmental measure, at the time those measures were taken, should retain standing to bring a claim, provided they did not otherwise relinquish their right to that claim.

In *KT Asia Investment Group B.V. v Republic of Kazakhstan* (ICSID Case No. ARB/09/8) (Award, 17 October 2013), the Tribunal found that there had not been an investment, based on the following facts:

1. The Claimant had made no contribution with respect to its alleged investment, nor was there any evidence on record that it had the intention or the ability to do so in the future.

2. The Claimant itself never had funds of any significance, other than a small amount to pay administrative expenses; and the only purpose for the incorporation of the Claimant was to hold some of the shares in BTA. Mr Ablyazov, the ultimate beneficial owner of the Claimant, remained the true owner of the shares.

3. The Claimant had purchased the shares at an undervalue and had never actually paid even this price for the shares. The payment of the shares was financed through loans made by the vendors of the shares, no security was given for those loans, and eventually the loans were written off and the lenders liquidated.

4. The investment was supposed to last a very short period of time – the business plan indicated that the shares were only to be held for a period of 3-4 weeks – the impact of the financial crisis hindered the financial placement, but this did not change the fact that the transaction was

never intended to involve a longer term allocation of resources.

In *Ambiente Ufficio S.p.A. and others v. Argentine Republic (formerly Giordano Alpi and others v. Argentine Republic)* (ICSID Case No. ARB/08/9) (Decision on Jurisdiction and Admissibility, 8 February 2013), after considering the territoriality requirement of the relevant bilateral investment treaty and how that applied to the investment at issue (sovereign bond instruments issued by Argentina and sold in the international markets, and security entitlements which had been purchased in the Italian market), a majority of the tribunal dismissed Argentina's argument that the investment was not made *"in the territory"* of the respondent as required by the BIT. The tribunal found that *"looking at the investment operation at stake as a whole and in terms of its economic realities, it is hard to imagine the investment's situs to be elsewhere than in Argentina."* Instruments such as sovereign bonds did not compare to a *"single commercial transaction"*, and should be protected if and to the extent that the contracting parties to the BIT intended those investments to be protected.

BIT Claim Checklist

In *Metal-Tech Ltd. v. Republic of Uzbekistan*, ICSID Case No. ARB/10/3 (Award, 4 October 2013), the Tribunal noted that compliance with the laws of the host State and good faith are not elements of an objective definition of *"investment"*, but States may choose to limit treaty protection to investments made in accordance with the laws of the host State. In the present case, *"implemented in accordance with the laws and regulations"* only required the investment to comply with local laws at the time of establishment (jurisdiction was denied in that case as the claimant had made payments to officials at the relevant time in breach of national anti-corruption laws).

Fair and Equitable Treatment?

What does this mean in practice?

How do you recognise unfair and inequitable treatment when you see it?

The meaning of fair and equitable treatment

There is no "standard" definition.

"Fair and equitable treatment" generally requires States *"to maintain stable and predictable investment environments consistent with reasonable investor expectations"*.

However, there is substantial room for exercise of discretion by the arbitral tribunal in each particular case. See for example:

1. *CME Czech Republic B.V. v. The Czech Republic*, UNCITRAL (Partial Award, 13 September 2001)

2. *Ronald S. Lauder v. The Czech Republic*, UNCITRAL (Final Award, 3 September 2001)

These cases essentially involved the same facts (nominally different parties and different BITs) (alleged interference with TV broadcast licence), yet:

1. *CME*: The Tribunal found that there had been a breach of the requirement for fair and equitable treatment, *"by evisceration of the arrangements in reliance upon which the foreign investor was induced to invest"*.

2. *Lauder*: The Tribunal found that there had been no breach of the requirement for fair and equitable treatment.

In *CMS Gas Transmission Company v. The Republic of Argentina*, ICSID Case No. ARB/01/8 (Award, 12 May 2005), involving a claim by an US investor following the massive currency devaluation and "pesification" by Argentina in the late 1990s, the tribunal held that Argentina had breached the requirement for fair and equitable treatment, by breaching the legitimate expectations of the investor.

Recent movement towards clarifying the standard

There have been several recent divergent, but not necessarily incompatible, attempts at clarification.

In *Swisslion DOO Skopje v. The Former Yugoslav Republic of Macedonia* (ICSID Case No. ARB/09/16) (Award, 6 July 2012), the

Tribunal held that it was unnecessary to engage in an extensive discussion of the FET standard, and approved the view that the: *"standard basically ensures that the foreign investor is not unjustly treated, with due regard to all surrounding circumstances, and that it is a means to guarantee justice to foreign investors."* (para. 273.) Examples of a breach of the FET standard could include:

1. Failure to engage with the investor on a timely basis (para. 276)

2. Failure to engage forthrightly with the investor (in *Swisslion*, the Tribunal was greatly concerned by the State's lack of detailed analysis and failure to engage the Claimant on the issue of the Claimant's compliance with a Share Sale Agreement)

3. Subjecting the investor to additional administrative proceedings outside of the contractual litigation (para. 296)

In *Occidental Petroleum Corporation and Occidental Exploration and Production Company v. The Republic of Ecuador* (ICSID Case No. ARB/06/11) (Award, 5 October 2012), the tribunal noted that *"the obligation for fair and equitable treatment has on several occasions been interpreted to import an obligation of proportionality"* (para. 404).

In *Bureau Veritas, Inspection, Valuation, Assessment and Control, BIVAC B.V. v. The Republic of Paraguay* (ICSID Case No. ARB/07/9) (Further Decision on Objections to Jurisdiction, 9 October 2012) held that in order to succeed in a claim alleging violation of the FET clause, the claimant must show that *"the conduct of Paraguay reflects an act of 'puissance publique', that is to say 'activity beyond that of an ordinary contracting party'"* (para. 211).

In *Bosh International, Inc and B&P Ltd Foreign Investments Enterprise v. Ukraine* (ICSID Case No. ARB/08/11) (Award, 25 October 2012) it was held that in order to establish a breach of the FET standard, the action or omission by the State needs to violate *"a certain threshold of propriety"* and among the relevant factors to be considered the tribunal referred to the host State's specific representations to the investor, lack of due process or transparency, harassment, coercion, abuse of power, bad faith, arbitrariness, discrimination or inconsistency (para. 212-217).

Also helpful are the considerations found in *Deutsche Bank AG v. Democratic Socialist Republic of Sri Lanka* (ICSID Case No. ARB/09/2) (Award, 31 October 2012) in which the tribunal noted a trend towards treating the content of autonomous FET clauses as *"not materially different from the content of the minimum standard of treatment in customary international law, as recognised by numerous arbitral tribunals and commentators"* (paras. 418-419).

The tribunal further distilled the standard:

1. protection of legitimate and reasonable expectations which have been relied upon by the investor to make the investment;

2. good faith conduct, although bad faith on the part of the State is not required for its violation;

3. conduct that is transparent, consistent and not discriminatory, that is, not based on unjustifiable distinctions or arbitrary;

4. conduct that does not offend judicial propriety, that complies with due process and the right to be heard (para. 420).

In *Rompetrol Group N.V. v Romania* (ICSID Case No. ARB/06/3) (Award, 6 May 2013), the Tribunal found that the cumulative effect of a series of wrongful acts were capable of amounting to a treaty breach even if, taken individually, they did not.

The *"cumulative"* approach was confirmed in *Gold Reserve Inc. v. Bolivarian Republic of Venezuela* (ICSID Case No. ARB(AF)/09/1) (Award, 22 September 2014), in which an ICSID tribunal awarded Gold Reserve Inc. over US$740 million in respect of Venezuela's breach of the fair and equitable treatment standard set out in the bilateral investment treaty between Venezuela and Canada. Even if a measure or conduct by the State, taken in isolation, does not rise to the level of a breach of the FET, such a breach may result from a series of circumstances or a combination of measures, particularly where the measures are part of a State policy aimed at gaining control of the object of the investment. In that case, the number, variety and seriousness of the breaches made the FET violation by Venezuela particularly egregious, and the compensation due to Gold Reserve for such breaches had to reflect the seriousness of the violation.

The relevance/irrelevance to the 'standard' of legitimate expectation

BIT Claim
Checklist

In *Electrabel S.A. v. Republic of Hungary* (ICSID Case No. ARB/07/19) (Decision on Jurisdiction, Applicable Law and Liability, 30 November 2012) the tribunal stated that while *"specific assurances may reinforce investor's expectations, such assurance is not always indispensable"* (para 7.78); that it was *"well-established that the host State is entitled to maintain a reasonable degree of regulatory flexibility to respond to changing circumstances in the public interest"*; and that, therefore, *"the requirement of fairness must not be understood as the immutability of the legal framework, but as implying that subsequent changes should be made fairly, consistently and predictably"* (para. 7.77).

Likewise, in *Ulysseas, Inc. v. The Republic of Ecuador* (UNCITRAL) (Final Award, 12 June 2012) it was stated that in the absence of specific promises or representations made by the State to the investor, the latter cannot have a legitimate expectation that there will be no changes in the host State's legal and economic framework (para. 217).

Similarly, in *Toto Costruzioni Generali S.p.A. v. The Republic of Lebanon* (ICSID Case No. ARB/07/12) (Award, 7 June 2012) it was stated that in the absence of a stabilisation clause or similar commitment, changes in the regulatory framework would be considered as breaches of the duty to grant FET *"only in case of a drastic or discriminatory change in the essential features of the transaction"* (para. 244).

23

In the later case of *Renée Rose Levy de Levi v. Republic of Peru* (ICSID Case No. ARB/10/17) (Award, 26 February 2014), the Tribunal noted that the legitimate expectations of an investor are linked to the standard of fair and equitable treatment. For an investor to make a decision on an investment, an important element usually considered is the stability of the country's legal system, although this does not mean a freezing of the legal system or making it impossible for the State to reform laws and other regulations in force at the time the investor made the investment.

In *Micula et al v. Romania* (ICSID Case No. ARB/05/20) (Award, 11 December 2013), the Tribunal found that the respondent's conduct does not need to be egregious to amount to a violation of the *"fair and equitable treatment"* standard, and such a clause should not be seen as equivalent to a stabilisation clause – the state's conduct will not contravene the standard where an investor's legitimate expectations are protected and the respondent's conduct is substantially and procedurally proper. Conduct that would violate the *"fair and equitable treatment"* standard includes that which is substantially improper (for example, conduct that is arbitrary, manifestly unreasonable, discriminatory or in bad faith). Transparency and consistency duties arising out of the *"fair and equitable treatment"* standard should be based on the circumstances in each case.

In *Gold Reserve Inc. v. Bolivarian Republic of Venezuela* (ICSID Case No. ARB(AF)/09/1), the tribunal observed that the investor's legitimate expectations are a central consideration in the analysis of whether treatment was fair and equitable in the circumstances. Legitimate expectations are based on undertakings and representations made explicitly or implicitly by the host State and are created when a State's conduct is such that an investor may reasonably rely on that conduct as being consistent. A reversal of assurances by the host State that have led to legitimate expectations will violate the principle of fair and equitable treatment.

Denial of justice

In *Liman Caspian Oil BV and NCL Dutch Investment BV v. Republic of Kazakhstan*, ICSID Case No. ARB/07/14 (Award, 22 June 2010), the Tribunal defined denial of justice as a fundamental failure of the court system and noted *"[s]uch failure is mainly to be held established in cases of major procedural errors such as lack of due process. The substantive outcome of a case can be relevant as an indication of lack of due process and thus can be considered as an element to prove denial of justice"* (para. 279).

The Tribunal's view was that the fair and equitable treatment standard under the Energy Charter Treaty was not limited to the minimum standard under customary international law, and the prohibition of denial of justice formed part of the fair and equitable treatment standard. It was possible that the actions of state courts may breach the fair and equitable treatment standard even if they do not amount to denial of justice.

BIT Claim
Checklist

However, contrast that approach with that taken in *Iberdrola Energía S.A. v. Republic of Guatemala* (ICSID Case No. ARB/09/5) (Award, 17 August 2012) in which the Tribunal reviewed the conduct of the host State on the basis of the concept of denial of justice in the current state of customary international law – suggesting that customary international law is the relevant standard (para. 427).

In *Robert Azinian, Kenneth Davitian, & Ellen Baca v. The United Mexican States*, ICSID Case No. ARB (AF)/97/2 (Award, 1 November 1999), concerning the termination of a waste management concession upheld by the Mexican courts, the tribunal found that the decision of the Mexican courts was based on relevant standards for annulling concessions under Mexican law. There was no evidence that the finding by the Mexican Courts was so insubstantial, bereft of basis in law so as to be arbitrary or malicious (and thus constitute a denial of justice).

More recently, in *Dan Cake (Portugal) S.A. v Hungary* (ICSID Case No. ARB/12/9) (Decision on Jurisdiction and Liability, 24

August 2015), an ICSID Tribunal (Prof. Pierre Mayer (President), sitting with Toby Landau QC and Jan Paulsson) found that a decision of the Hungarian bankruptcy court (which, it was not disputed, was under international law attributable to the State itself) was a violation of the obligation to treat the investor in a fair and equitable manner which took the form of a denial of justice.

Has there been expropriation of the investment?

There are various treaty based restrictions on expropriation (Art. 1110 NAFTA, Art. 13 Energy Charter Treaty, BITs, S.712(g) American Restatement 3rd of the Foreign Relations Law).

The general rule is that investment shall not be expropriated or nationalised or subjected to measures having the effect equivalent to expropriation or nationalisation except:

1. for a public purpose

2. in a non-discriminatory manner

3. in accordance with due process

4. against prompt, adequate and effective compensation

Compensation may still be awarded in respect of an expropriation which is a lawful expropriation. In *Mobil Corporation, Venezuela Holdings, B.V., Mobil Cerro Negro Holding, Ltd., Mobil Venezolana de Petróleos Holdings, Inc., Mobil Cerro Negro, Ltd., and Mobil Venezolana de Petróleos, Inc. v. Venezuela*, ICSID Case No. ARB/07/27 (Award, 9 October 2014), an ICSID tribunal awarded Mobil over US$1.6 billion in damages arising from the direct expropriation of Mobil's investment in various oil assets in Venezuela, despite finding that the expropriation had been lawful. In particular, the Tribunal noted that:

1. The measures taken by Venezuela had complied with the due process requirements of Article 6 of the Netherlands-Venezuela BIT. The process implemented by Venezuela in connection with the passing of the laws (the purpose of which was to create new mixed

companies in which the State would own more than 50% of the shares) provided for negotiations between the State and oil companies, and therefore enabled the participating companies to weigh their interests and make decisions during a reasonable period of time.

2. There was no evidence that the expropriation had been carried out contrary to undertakings given by Venezuela to the Claimants.

3. The mere fact that an investor had not received compensation did not in itself render an expropriation unlawful.

4. An offer of compensation may have been made to the investor and, in such a case, the legality of the expropriation would depend on the terms of that offer.

5. In order to decide whether an expropriation was lawful or not in the absence of payment of compensation, a tribunal must consider the facts of the case.

6. As the expropriation was not held to be an unlawful expropriation, compensation was to be determined at the time of the expropriation rather than at the time of the award (in contrast to *ConocoPhillips Petrozuata B.V., ConocoPhillips Hamaca B.V. and ConocoPhillips Gulf of Paria B.V. v. Venezuela* (ICSID Case No. ARB/07/30), in which an ICSID tribunal, in a decision dated 3 September 2013, held that the expropriation was unlawful and accordingly compensation was to be assessed in a later hearing as at the date of the award).

What sort of state conduct constitutes an expropriation?

Key Test: Whether action of a state deprives investor of the whole or significant part of investment (substantial deprivation test).

However, deprivation is not the determinative factor for expropriation.

BIT Claim
Checklist

Bona fide acts of state, such as general taxation, regulation for public health and other exercise of state police powers if not discriminatory, do not constitute expropriation.

The key question is therefore when does conduct of state cross the line that separates valid regulatory activity from expropriation?

In *Vannessa Ventures Ltd. v. Bolivarian Republic of Venezuela* (ICSID Case No. ARB(AF)/04/6) (Award, 16 January 2013), the Tribunal held that contractual rights are capable of being expropriated. In order to amount to an expropriation under international law, it is necessary that the conduct of the State should go beyond that which an ordinary contracting party could adopt – "legitimate contractual responses" to contractual breaches will not suffice.

Note:

1. The form and intent of a government measure will always be important but not always decisive.

2. There is no need to show obvious benefit to the Host State.

3. Outright expropriation is relatively easy to recognise – State takes over a business or nationalises an entire industry (fairly uncommon).

4. What amounts to expropriation is largely fact driven.

5. "Creeping"/"regulatory" expropriation is more likely to be seen where the investor's ability to conduct business is effectively undermined by regulations/State acts or omissions.

Further, while compensation for expropriation is not required at the moment of expropriation, parties must engage in good faith negotiations to fix the compensation in terms of the standard set if a payment satisfactory to the investor is not proposed at the outset (*ConocoPhillips Petrozuata B.V., ConocoPhillips Hamaca B.V. and ConocoPhillips Gulf of Paria B.V.*

v. Bolivarian Republic of Venezuela (ICSID Case No. ARB/07/30) (Decision on Jurisdiction and Merits, 3 September 2013)).

Direct expropriation

In *Burlington Resources Inc. v. Republic of Ecuador* (ICSID Case No. ARB/08/5) (Decision on Liability, 14 December 2012) the tribunal held that a governmental measure would constitute direct expropriation if:

1. the measure deprived the investor of his investment;

2. the deprivation was permanent; and

3. the deprivation found no justification under the police powers doctrine (para. 506).

Indirect expropriation

Again in *Burlington Resources Inc. v. Republic of Ecuador* (ICSID Case No. ARB/08/5) (Decision on Liability, 14 December 2012) the tribunal held that the measure alleged to constitute indirect expropriation must (as set out in past decisions) have resulted in substantial deprivation (para. 396).

The tribunal explained that a loss of management or control over the investment was not a necessary element of substantial deprivation: *"what appears to be decisive, in assessing whether there is a substantial deprivation, is the loss of the economic value or economic viability of the investment. The loss of viability does not necessarily imply a loss of management or control. What matters is the capacity to earn a commercial return"* (para. 397).

The tribunal further noted that the criterion of loss of the economic use or viability of the investment applied to *"the investment as a whole"* – a windfall profit tax could not be tantamount to expropriation: *"[B]y definition, such a tax would appear not to have an impact upon the investment as a whole, but only on a portion of the profits. On the assumption that its effects are in line with its name, a windfall profits tax is unlikely to result in the expropriation of an investment"* (para. 404).

29

In *Electrabel S.A. v. Republic of Hungary* (ICSID Case No. ARB/07/19) (Decision on Jurisdiction, Applicable Law and Liability, 30 November 2012) the tribunal held that to prove indirect expropriation, the claimant must prove that its investment lost all significant economic value following early termination etc. (para. 6.53). Furthermore, *"both in applying the wording of Article 13(1) ECT and under international law, the test for expropriation is applied to the relevant investment as a whole, even if different parts may separately qualify as investments for jurisdictional purposes"* (para. 6.58).

The decision in *Renta 4 S.V.S.A., et al v. The Russian Federation* (SCC No. 24/2007) (Award, 20 July 2012) emphasised that indirect expropriation must be deduced from a pattern of conduct, observing its conception, implementation, and effects, even if the intention to expropriate is disavowed at every step (para. 45).

In *Metalclad Corporation v. The United Mexican States*, ICSID Case No. ARB(AF)/97/1 (Award, 30 August 2000), the investor obtained the necessary federal permit to operate landfill, but the local municipality subsequently denied a construction permit forcing the facility to close. Later, the State Governor issued an ecological decree (ostensibly for the preservation of cactus in the area) which had the effect of barring operation of the facility. The tribunal found that the measure was tantamount to expropriation – by tolerating and acquiescing in actions of municipal authorities which prevented operation of landfill despite approval of federal authorities; and passing of the ecological decree.

In *CME Czech Republic B.V. v. The Czech Republic*, UNCITRAL (Partial Award, 13 September 2001), Lauder, a US investor, invested in CME, a Dutch company, which in turn invested in a Czech company which was to hold a broadcasting licence and operate a television station. There was a public outcry at foreign ownership of television broadcasting after the award of the licence. A new business agreement was concluded as a result of the involvement of the Czech Media Council whereby CNTS (a joint venture) was set up to hold the broadcasting licence. The Tribunal held that this constituted indirect expropriation on two grounds – (1) the Media Council deprived CNTS of exclusive use of the broadcasting licence; and (2) the Media Council forced changes in the relationship between CNTS and the joint venture partner benefitting the joint venture partner. The State's actions, the Tribunal held, coerced CME to abandon the legal security for its investment in the Czech Republic. However, note that the *Lauder* Tribunal found (on the same facts) that there was no expropriation.

In *Pope & Talbot Inc. v. The Government of Canada*, UNCITRAL (Interim Award, 26 June 2000), the relevant test was said to be is the interference sufficiently restrictive to support a conclusion that property was taken?   In that case, the Investor was able to continue to export and to earn profit from those exports; remained in control of the investment including day-to-day operations. Therefore, there was no substantial deprivation of right. The factors referred to in *Pope & Talbot* (whether: (a) The investment has been nationalized or the measure is confiscatory; (b) The investor remains in control of the investment and directs its day-to-day operations, or whether the State has taken over such management and control; (c) The State now supervises the work of employees of the Investment; and (d) The State takes the proceeds of the company's sales) were cited with approval in *Tidewater Investment SRL and Tidewater Caribe, C.A. v. Bolivarian Republic of Venezuela* (ICSID Case No. ARB/10/5) (Award, 13 March 2015).

BIT Claim Checklist

In *S.D. Myers v. Canada*, UNCITRAL (Partial Award, 13 November 2000), the Canadian government closed the border to transportation of PCB hazardous waste to the detriment of S.D. Myers whose Canadian operation engaged in sale of such waste to USA based entities. The tribunal held that Canada had not acted for a legitimate environmental purpose and was motivated by a protectionist desire to favour Canadian firms engaged in waste remediation. Creeping expropriation was defined as *"a lasting removal of the ability of an owner to make use of its economic rights"*. In this case, the temporary closure of border to PCB transport was not expropriation (but it was a breach of minimum standard of treatment).

In *CMS Gas Transmission Company v. The Republic of Argentina*, ICSID Case No. ARB/01/8 (Award, 12 May 2005), a licence granted to a gas transportation company provided that the tariff was to be calculated in USD, converted into pesos and indexed to US PPI. In 1999 Argentina temporarily suspended PPI adjustment, and subsequently suspended it permanently (not for exports). In 2000 a court injunction suspended the license pending a challenge to the legality of the PPI adjustment. In 2001, an Emergency Law set the exchange rate 1 peso to 1 dollar.

The tribunal held that there was no indirect expropriation as per the substantial deprivation test. Applying *Pope & Talbot* and *Metalclad*, the tribunal held that the investor was in control of the investment, the day-to-day management of business, and was able to export. Note: Argentina commenced ICSID annulment proceedings, and was granted a stay of execution of the Award in the interim. By a decision dated 21 August 2007, the Tribunal substantially dismissed Argentina's annulment application, although the Tribunal did partially annul the Award insofar as it had held that Argentina had acted in breach of the "umbrella clause" contained in Article II(2)(c) of the BIT (Argentina's duty to observe any obligation it may have entered into with regard to investments).

In *Franck Charles Arif v. Republic of Moldova* (ICSID Case No. ARB/11/23) (Award, 8 April 2013), it was held that significant legal insecurity in respect of the claimant's investment could not amount to an expropriation of the claimant's investment where, for the moment, the claimant had not been deprived of the use and benefit of his investment (even where such deprivation appeared imminent).

Breach of full protection and security

In *Gold Reserve Inc. v. Bolivarian Republic of Venezuela* (ICSID Case No. ARB(AF)/09/1), the Tribunal dismissed Gold

Reserve's claim under Article II(2) of the BIT (providing for the duty to accord full protection and security to investments). While some investment treaty tribunals have extended the concept of full protection and security to an obligation to provide regulatory and legal protections, the more traditional, and commonly accepted view is that this standard of treatment refers to protection against physical harm to persons and property. There was no suggestion in the present case that Venezuela failed to protect Gold Reserve's investment from physical harm, and therefore no breach of the full protection and security standard occurred.

Are there Most-Favoured Nation Provisions Implications?

There is evidence of divergent approaches to the interpretation and application of these provisions in the recent decisions. The scope and impact of the MFN clauses have been a source of much debate, with over 20 arbitral tribunals handing down conflicting decisions on the question of whether such a clause can be used to take advantage of more favourable dispute resolution provisions, accompanied by a significant amount of academic discussion and commentary.

In *Garanti Koza LLP v. Turkmenistan* (ICSID Case No. ARB/11/20) (Decision on Jurisdiction, 3 July 2013), the Tribunal described the issue of MFN clauses as *"a fiercely contested no-man's land in international law"*.

Some tribunals have questioned the implications of the application (or non-application) of the MFN clause, and in particular, whether the MFN clause goes to the Tribunal's jurisdiction or the admissibility of the Claimant's claims (see, for example, *Kilic Insaat Ithalat Ihracat Sanayi ve Ticaret Anonim Sirketi v. Turkmenistan* (ICSID Case No. ARB/10/1) (Award, 2 July 2013 cf Separate Opinion of William Park, 20 May 2013).

In *Teinver S.A., Transportes de Cercanías S.A. and Autobuses Urbanos del Sur S.A. v. The Argentine Republic* (ICSID Case No. ARB/09/1) (Decision on Jurisdiction, 21 December 2012), the majority of the tribunal held that claimant could rely on the

MFN clause found in the Argentina-Spain BIT to make use of the (more favourable) dispute resolution provisions contained in Article 13 of the Argentina-Australia BIT. The tribunal noted that the broad *"all matters"* language of the MFN clause was unambiguously inclusive (para. 186).

In contrast, in *ICS Inspection and Control Services Limited (United Kingdom) v. The Republic of Argentina* (UNCITRAL, PCA Case No. 2010-9) (Award on Jurisdiction, 10 February 2012), the tribunal found that the MFN clause in Article 3 of the Argentina-UK BIT did not apply in such a way as to permit the claimant to avail itself of the dispute resolution provisions of the Argentina- Lithuania BIT (para. 280).

The tribunal noted:

1. *"a State's consent to arbitration shall not be presumed in the face of ambiguity [and] where a claimant fails to prove consent with sufficient certainty, jurisdiction will be declined"* (para. 280).

2. the term *"treatment"*, in the absence of any contrary stipulation in the treaty itself, was most likely meant by the two Contracting Parties to refer only to the legal regime to be respected by the host State in conformity with its international obligations, conventional or customary, while the settlement of disputes remained an entirely distinct issue, covered by a separate and specific treaty provision (para. 296).

3. reference to *"treatment in its territory"* in the MFN clause clearly imposed a territorial limitation, which consequently excluded international arbitration proceedings from the scope of the MFN clause (para. 296).

Similarly, in *Daimler Financial Services AG v. Argentine Republic* (ICSID Case No. ARB/05/1) (Award, 22 August 2012), the majority determined that the language of the Argentina-Germany BIT's MFN clause was territorially limited, that *"treatment"* was intended by the parties to refer only to treatment of the investment, and that the BIT did not extend MFN treatment to *"all matters"* subject to the BIT (paras. 224, 230-231, 236).

In *Kilic Insaat Ithalat Ihracat Sanayi ve Ticaret Anonim Sirketi v. Turkmenistan* (ICSID Case No. ARB/10/1) (Award, 2 July 2013), Kilic argued that the MFN clause in the BIT overrode the mandatory provisions which required disputes to be submitted to the national courts. Turkmenistan asserted that Kilic's failure to comply with the dispute resolution processes deprived the Tribunal of jurisdiction and the mandatory requirements were not overridden by virtue of the MFN clause.

The Tribunal held that the MFN clause did not encompass or apply to the Turkey-Turkmenistan BIT's dispute resolution provisions so as to permit Kilic to rely on the dispute resolution provisions of the Switzerland-Turkmenistan BIT. Accordingly, the Tribunal found that it did not have jurisdiction over this arbitration, unless Kilic was excused from mandatory prior recourse to Turkmenistan's courts on grounds that such recourse would be obviously futile.

In contrast, in *Garanti Koza LLP v. Turkmenistan* (ICSID Case No. ARB/11/20) (Decision on Jurisdiction, 3 July 2013), Turkmenistan alleged that Garanti Koza LLP could not use the MFN clause to avoid the specific requirement contained in the BIT that in order for a dispute to be submitted to ICSID, an agreement to ICSID arbitration between the investor and the BIT's Contracting Party must exist given the requirement in the BIT that the parties must choose between UNCITRAL, ICC or ICSID arbitration.

Turkmenistan had argued that, while an MFN clause may possibly be used to overcome a qualifying condition, such as a waiting period, in the dispute resolution clause of a BIT (as was the case in *Maffezini v. Spain*) it may not be used to *"import"* the State's *"consent to a different arbitration system"* from one treaty into another as Garanti Koza LLP was attempting to do in this case. The Tribunal disagreed with this interpretation, and held that the Article 3(3) of the BIT expressly provided that the MFN treatment applied to the dispute resolution provisions of the BIT.

In a Dissenting Opinion, Arbitrator Laurence Boisson de Chazournes asserted that finding in favour of Garanti Koza LLP *"would involve a forum shopping attitude,"* *"running against the fundamental principles of international adjudication,"* to bypass the consent requirement. The arbitrator held that for the MFN clause to apply to the dispute resolution provisions, the parties must first be in a dispute resolution relationship – and in this case, the parties were not.

Are there "Umbrella Clauses"/Implications?

Again, in the application of these clauses there appears to be a lack of lack of consensus. Thus, in *SGS Société Générale de Surveillance S.A. v. The Republic of Paraguay* (ICSID Case No. ARB/07/29) (Award, 10 February 2012), it was held that there was nothing in Article 11 of the Paraguay-Switzerland BIT that stated or implied that a government would only fail to observe its commitments if it abuses its sovereign authority (para. 91); and consequently that if the respondent failed to observe any of its contractual commitments, it breached Article 11 and no further examination of whether respondent's actions are properly characterized as *"sovereign"* or *"commercial"* in nature was necessary (para. 95).

On the other hand, in *Bosh International, Inc and B&P Ltd Foreign Investments Enterprise v. Ukraine* (ICSID Case No. ARB/08/11) (Award, 25 October 2012), it was held that the term "Party" in Article II(3)(c) of the Ukraine-US BIT referred to any situation where the Party was acting qua State, meaning that where the conduct of entities could be attributed to the host State, such entities should be considered to be "the Party" for the purposes of Article II(3)(c) (paras. 243 and 246).

More recently, in *Micula et al v. Romania* (ICSID Case No. ARB/05/20) (Award, 11 December 2013), it was held that depending on the language used in the BIT, the umbrella clause may cover obligations of any nature, regardless of their source (both contractual and non-contractual obligations).

Are there explicitly incorporated procedural requirements?

Some treaties require that a claimant under the BIT must comply with certain procedural requirements before commencing arbitration. Such requirements can include the obligation to attempt to resolve the situation amicably, and commence proceedings in the local courts. Whether such provisions have been complied with is often a subject of much dispute if an arbitration is commenced, particularly if a claimant has opted not to commence or complete the obligation on the grounds that they consider it would be futile.

In *ICS Inspection and Control Services Limited (United Kingdom) v. The Republic of Argentina* (UNCITRAL, PCA Case No. 2010-9) (Award on Jurisdiction, 10 February 2012), the tribunal noted that the trend in public international law (as evidenced for example in the recent decision of the ICJ in the Case concerning Application of the International Convention on the Elimination of All Forms of Racial Discrimination (*Georgia v. Russian Federation*) (International Court of Justice), Decision on Preliminary Objections, 1 April 2011, paras. 133-135) has clearly favoured the strict application of procedural prerequisites (para. 250).

The tribunal also held that the 18-month recourse-to-local-courts requirement constitutes a condition to the respondent State's consent to arbitration (paras. 258-262). Moreover, the tribunal decided that it could not ignore the 18-month recourse-to-local-courts requirement on the basis that the litigation would be futile or inefficient – stressing that it could not *"create exceptions to treaty rules where these are merely based upon an assessment of the wisdom of the policy in question, having no basis in either the treaty text or in any supplementary interpretive source, however desirable such policy considerations might be seen to be in the abstract"* (paras. 267-269).

Consequently, the tribunal found that it lacked jurisdiction due to the claimant's failure to comply with the mandatory 18-month "recourse to local courts" requirement set forth in Article 8 of the Argentina-UK BIT. Similar reasoning was adopted in *Daimler Financial Services AG v. Argentine Republic* (ICSID Case No. ARB/05/1) (Award, 22 August 2012).

However, on an identical provision in Article X(1) of the Argentina-Spain BIT it was held in *Teinver S.A., Transportes de Cercanías S.A. and Autobuses Urbanos del Sur S.A. v. The Argentine Republic* (ICSID Case No. ARB/09/1) (Decision on Jurisdiction, 21 December 2012) that as long as the local proceedings dealt with the same subject-matter as the one brought to international arbitration, the treaty requirement is met (para. 112).

Equally, the tribunal noted that the underlying BIT permits either party (including the respondent State) to initiate the domestic litigation for the recourse-to-local-courts requirement to be fulfilled (paras. 133-135).

In *Philip Morris Brand Sàrl (Switzerland), Philip Morris Products S.A. (Switzerland) and Abal Hermanos S.A. (Uruguay) v. Oriental Republic of Uruguay* (ICSID Case No. ARB/10/7)(Decision on Jurisdiction, 2 July 2013), the Tribunal held that a dispute before domestic courts under the local remedy requirement does not need to have the same legal basis or cause of action as the dispute brought in the subsequent arbitration, provided that both disputes involve *"substantially similar facts and relate to investments as this term is defined by the BIT."*

In *Ömer Dede and Serdar Elhüseyni v. Romania* (ICSID Case No. ARB/10/22) (Procedural Order No. 1 and Award of the Tribunal, 5 September 2013), the Tribunal held that the most reasonable test for implementing the ordinary meaning of the procedural requirements in the Treaty at issue required that disputes brought before local courts be of a nature that permits resolution to substantially the same extent as if brought before an international arbitral tribunal pursuant to an investment treaty.

In *Tulip Real Estate and Development Netherlands B.V. v. Republic of Turkey* (ICSID Case No. ARB/11/28), (Decision on Bifurcated Jurisdictional Issue, 5 March 2013), the Tribunal held that compliance with a requirement to seek consultations and negotiations for one year until date of notification of the dispute was not a *"mere statement of aspiration"* but was an essential element of the respondent's consent to arbitration, and therefore a pre-condition to the jurisdiction of the tribunal under the terms of the relevant BIT.

Is there sufficient evidence to make out a prima facie case of breach of a BIT?

In *Iberdrola Energía S.A. v. Republic of Guatemala* (ICSID Case No. ARB/09/5) (Award, 17 August 2012), it was stated, whilst considering the terms of the Guatemala-Spain BIT, that such treaties do not give *"general consent to submit any kind of dispute or difference related to investments [...], but only those related to violations of substantive provisions of the treaty itself."* (para. 306); and an international tribunal will only have jurisdiction if the claimant establishes *"that the facts it alleged, if proven, could constitute a violation of the Treaty"* (paras. 323-373).

In relation to the burden of proof and requirement of proving the Claimant's case, see the (somewhat scathing) criticism of the Claimant's pleading in the ICSID Tribunal's decision in the case of *Telenor Mobile Communications A.S. v. The Republic of Hungary*, ICSID Case No. ARB/04/15 (Award, 13 September 2006), where the Claimant had failed to establish (at the threshold level of jurisdiction) a prima facie case of expropriation in relation to provision of telecommunication services.

In *Chevron Corporation and Texaco Petroleum Corporation v. The Republic of Ecuador* (UNCITRAL, PCA Case No. 2009-23) (Third Interim Award on Jurisdiction and Admissibility, 27 February 2012), the Tribunal held that for the purposes of considering a respondent's jurisdictional objections, it was necessary for the tribunal to decide whether or not, if the facts alleged by the claimants are assumed to be true, the challenged conduct would be capable of constituting breaches of the BIT. The assumption of truth could be reversed if such factual pleadings were *"incredible, frivolous, vexatious or otherwise advanced by the Claimant in bad faith"* (para. 4.6). It was not required that a chance of success greater than 51% should be made out, just that the case was *"decently arguable"* or possessed of *"a reasonable possibility as pleaded"* (para. 4.8).

Is there evidence of a "knock out" point such as the payment of a bribe?

See the decision of the ICSID Tribunal in *World Duty Free Company Limited v. The Republic of Kenya*, ICSID Case No. ARB/00/7 (Award, 4 October 2006), where the Claimant (alleging, inter alia, that its investment in construction of duty free complexes in Kenya had been expropriated) deployed evidence to the effect that senior Kenyan officials had been bribed in 1989 by its personnel, to obtain the contract pursuant to which its investment had been made.

Perhaps unsurprisingly, (because it is extremely rare for a party to advance facts relating to payment of a bribe - unless it is seeking to avoid contractual responsibilities/legal claims), the Tribunal dismissed the claim.

In *Jan Oostergetel and Theodora Laurentius v. The Slovak Republic*, UNCITRAL (Final Award, 23 April 2012), the Tribunal noted that *"For obvious reasons, it is generally difficult to bring positive proof of corruption. Yet, corruption can also be proven by circumstantial evidence."*

What is the claim worth - what are "just and equitable" damages?

For either breach of the fair and equitable standard, or an expropriation, the most likely remedy to be awarded by the tribunal is damages. Different considerations apply in respect of fair and equitable standard and expropriation.

The exact quantum of the claim will depend in part on the valuation measure chosen by the Tribunal.

Fair and equitable standard

Investment treaties typically set out an explicit standard of compensation for expropriation cases only, which require prompt, adequate and effective compensation equal to the fair market value of the expropriated investment. When non-expropriatory treaty violations are found, damages have been awarded in accordance with the rules of international law that require "full compensation".

In a number of cases concerning FET breaches, this resulted in an award of the fair market value of the investment calculated by reference to future cash flows.

Lemire v Ukraine (ICSID Case No ARB/06/18) (Award, 28 March 2011) considered the standard to be applied in cases of breach of fair and equitable standard. The Tribunal in that case noted that it is generally admitted that in situations where the breach of the FET standard does not lead to total loss of the investment, the purpose of the compensation must be to place the investor in the same pecuniary position in which it would have been if the respondent had not violated the BIT.

In *Gold Reserve Inc. v. Bolivarian Republic of Venezuela* (ICSID Case No. ARB(AF)/09/1), in which damages were awarded for breach of the fair and equitable standard, the Tribunal held that the number, variety and seriousness of the breaches made the FET violation by Venezuela particularly egregious, and the compensation due to Gold Reserve for such breaches had to reflect the seriousness of the violation.

Expropriation

In *Chorzów Factory (Germany v Poland) (Merits)* (1928) PCIJ Rep Ser A No 17, the Tribunal distinguished between lawful and unlawful takings and held that, in case of lawful expropriation, the damage suffered must be repaired through the "*payment of fair compensation*" or "*the just price of what was expropriated*" at the time of the expropriation, meaning the "*value of the undertaking at the moment of dispossession, plus interest to the day of payment*"; while "*in case of unlawful expropriation, international law provides for restitutio in integrum or, if impossible, its monetary equivalent at the time of the judgment"*. Under the *Chorzów* rule, a claimant is free to request whatever it believes will serve to re-establish the situation as if the wrongful act never occurred – ie, in addition to the loss of future profits, investors have claimed, inter alia, moral damages, incidental expenses (e.g. costs of removing the personnel from a foreign country, costs incurred in liquidating the company established to operate the investment) and legal fees.

The Iran-United States Claims Tribunal distinguished between lawful and unlawful expropriations in the case of Amoco International Finance Corporation (*Amoco International Finance Corporation v. Iran*, Interlocutory Award of 14 July 1987, Iran-United States Claims Tribunal Reports (1987-II), § 192): *"[A] clear distinction must be made between lawful and unlawful expropriations, since the rules applicable to the compensation to be paid by the expropriating State differ according to the legal characterization of the taking."*

UNCTAD states that while in theory there is a distinction between compensation for lawful expropriations and reparation for unlawful ones, the typical approach is to award an investment's fair market value, regardless of the type of expropriation. See the decision of the ICSID Tribunal in *PSEG Global, Inc., The North American Coal Corporation, and Konya Ingin Electrik Üretim ve Ticaret Limited Sirketi v. Republic of Turkey*, ICSID Case No. ARB/02/5 (Award, 19 January 2007) (at pages 72 to 87) for the approach to fair market value and loss of profits.

More recently, in *Tidewater Investment SRL and Tidewater Caribe, C.A. v. Bolivarian Republic of Venezuela* (ICSID Case No. ARB/10/5) (Award (March 13, 2015)), the Tribunal (having found that the expropriation was lawful) considered the relevance and application of the compensation standard in the determination of the lawfulness of the expropriation. In the view of the Tribunal, an expropriation wanting only a determination of compensation by an international tribunal was not to be treated as an illegal expropriation. On calculating the value of the compensation, the Tidewater tribunal:

1. Observed that the *"essential difference between [lawful and unlawful expropriation] is that compensation for a lawful expropriation is fair compensation represented by the value of the undertaking at the moment of dispossession and reparation in case of unlawful expropriation is restitution in kind or its monetary equivalent."*

2. Endorsed the World Bank Guidelines as providing reasonable guidance as to the content of the standard chosen by the States Parties to the BIT as the standard of compensation to be applied in cases of lawful compensation, where the investment constituted a going concern at the time of the taking. Absent agreement of the parties, the Guidelines define the fair market value as to be determined *'according to reasonable criteria related to the market value of the investment, i.e., in an amount that a willing buyer would normally pay to a willing seller after taking into account the nature of the investment, the circumstances in which it would operate in the future and its specific characteristics, including the period in which it has been in existence, the proportion of tangible assets in the total investment and other relevant factors pertinent to the specific circumstances of each case'*.

3. Noted that while the compensation in a lawful expropriation was to be considered as at immediately before the expropriation, this does not mean that the valuation would be unconcerned with future prospects:

   • as the World Bank Guidelines themselves confirm, the factors that a willing buyer would itself take into account on the purchase of such an investment necessarily include *'the circumstances in which it would operate in the future'*; and

   • the Tribunal is not required to shut its eyes to events subsequent to the date of injury, if these shed light

43

in more concrete terms on the value applicable at the date of injury or validate the reasonableness of a valuation made at that date.

The Yukos Cases

In addition to the much publicised arbitration proceedings in the Permanent Court of Arbitration brought by the majority shareholders in Yukos pursuant to the Energy Charter Treaty which resulted in an award of approximately US$50 billion against the Russian Federation in compensation for losses suffered as a result of unlawful expropriation of Yukos' assets[1], various minority shareholders brought claims against Russia pursuant to BITs. *RosInvest Co UK Ltd v The Russian Federation* (Final Award, 12 September 2010) and *Quasar de Valores SICAV SA v The Russian Federation* (Award, 20 July 2012) concerned claims brought pursuant to the UK-Russia BIT and Spain-Russia BIT respectively.

Interestingly, the two Tribunals in *RosInvest* and *Quasar* took different approaches to the assessment of damages:

1. The *RosInvest* Tribunal considered that because the claimant had known of Yukos' difficulties when it made its investment, it would be unjust to award damages on the basis of a best case valuation (i.e. based on a hypothetical value of Yukos' shares but for the actions of the Russian Federation). Further, expert evidence

---

[1] In the proceedings brought under the Energy Charter Treaty (*Yukos Universal Ltd (Isle of Man) v The Russian Federation, PCA Case No. AA 227*), an arbitral tribunal constituted at the Permanent Court of Arbitration (The Hon. L. Yves Fortier QC (Chairman), Dr. Charles Poncet and Judge Stephen M. Schwebel) handed down a Final Award on 18 July 2014. By the Final Award, the Tribunal found that the Russian Federation's actions had breached its obligations under the Energy Charter Treaty. However, the Tribunal also held that the energy company's misuse of tax-free zones within Russia merited a finding of contributory fault on the part of Yukos – resulting in a (somewhat puzzling) 25% reduction to the damages to be awarded to the claimants. Accordingly, the Russian Federation was ordered to pay a reduced sum of US$50 billion in compensation. Consider and contrast with the approach of the European Court of Human Rights in applying Article 1 (Protocol 1) ECHR in *OAO Neftyanaya Kompaniya Yukos v Russia* (14902/04) [2014] ECHR 853.

(accepted by the Tribunal) showed that, at the time of the investment, the markets had already taken into account the effect of the Russian Federation's measures against Yukos and so the markets had been a true reflection of the likelihood that Yukos would survive profitably beyond the enforcement of those measures;

2. However, the *Quasar* Tribunal considered the approach in *RosInvest* too simple. It was not simply a case of determining the underlying value of Yukos' assets – the prospects of those assets were capable of being affected by a very wide range of factors that were not a matter of science. The Tribunal held that the Russian Federation would be *"ordered to pay for what it took, valued at the time of the taking, and without any consideration of the benefits it may since have enjoyed by reason of its actions – whether in terms of pure revenue or in the achievement of policy objectives"* (para. 214).

Valuation methods

Once the basis on which the damages have been assessed has been established, the Tribunal may have to decide the valuation of such loss. Expert evidence is usually provided on this point.

Tribunals have used a number of different methods to calculate value of breach of fair and equitable standard/ expropriation in previous cases:

1. Discounted cash flow value - Receipts realistically expected from the enterprise in each future year of its economic life as reasonably projected minus that year's expected cash expenditure, after discounting this net cash flow for each year by a factor which reflects the time value of money, expected inflation and the risk associated with such cash flow under realistic circumstances.

2. Replacement value - Cash amount required to replace the individual assets of the enterprise in their actual state as of the date of the taking.

3. Book value - Difference between the enterprise's assets and liabilities as recorded on its financial statements or the amount at which the taken tangible assets appear on the balance sheet of the enterprise, representing their cost after deducting accumulated depreciation in accordance with generally accepted accounting principles.

Examples of the use of such methods are as follows:

1. In *Tidewater Investment SRL and Tidewater Caribe, C.A. v. Bolivarian Republic of Venezuela* (ICSID Case No. ARB/10/5) (Award 13 March 2015)), valuation methods based on the liquidation value of the assets of the enterprise, or the book value of those would likely only be appropriate, as the World Bank Guidelines point out, where the enterprise was not a proven going concern. In that case, the DCF method was held to be the most appropriate valuation method.

2. In *Bernardus Henricus Funnekotter and others v. Republic of Zimbabwe*, ICSID Case No. ARB/05/6 (Award, 22 April 2009), the Tribunal determined that the host government had failed to provide compensation (which must represent the *"genuine value of the investment"*) in breach of the underlying BIT and thus proceeded in evaluating the damages suffered by the investors on the basis of the market value at the date of dispossession. The tribunal observed that *"under general international law as well as under the BIT, investors have a right to indemnities corresponding to the value of their investment, independently of the origin and past success of their investment, as well as of the number and aim of the expropriations done."*

3. *El Paso Energy International Company v. The Argentine Republic*, ICSID Case No. ARB/03/15 (Award, 31 October 2011) and *Lemire v Ukraine* (ICSID Case No ARB/06/18) (Award, 28 March 2011) both used the Discounted Cash Flow Method, although in *Lemire*, the Tribunal, given the number of assumptions, tested the results reached via the DCF method against other parameters, including the

"amounts invested", *"risk environment"* and *"comparable transactions"*.

4. *Impregilo S.p.A. v. Argentine Republic*, ICSID Case No. ARB/07/17 (Award, 21 June 2011) – The tribunal determined the damages to be paid by Argentina on the basis of a reasonable estimate of the loss that may have been caused to *Impregilo*, on the grounds that the responsibility for the failure of the concession was shared by both the foreign investor and Argentina.

Additional
Considerations

47

ADDITIONAL CONSIDERATIONS

Preliminary/provisional measures

A number of cases have addressed the issue of preliminary measures and availability of security for costs. Some key points observed from these cases (as will be discussed further below) include:

1. Where a jurisdictional challenge is made in respect of an application for provisional measures, the Tribunal is only required to be prima facie satisfied that it has jurisdiction over the dispute. Similarly, the Tribunal should be satisfied that there is a prima facie case on the merits (although the Tribunal should not pre-judge the issues).

2. Provisional measures should only be granted in situations of absolute necessity and urgency, in order to protect rights that could, absent these measures, be definitely lost.

3. The requesting party has the burden of showing why the requested provisional measures are necessary and should be ordered by the Tribunal.

4. The party requesting provisional measures must demonstrate that, if the requested measures are not granted, there is a material risk of serious or irreparable injury. There are variations in approach or the precise wording used by the ICSID tribunals as to whether this requirement is that of *"irreparable"* harm, or whether a demonstration of *"serious"* harm will suffice.

5. Security for costs will rarely be ordered, and only in the most exceptional of circumstances.

Phoenix Action, Ltd. v. The Czech Republic, ICSID Case No. ARB/06/5 (Decision on Provisional Measures, 6 April 2007)

The Claimant was an Israeli Company entirely owned by one individual. The Claimant became sole shareholder of two Czech companies in December 2002. The Czech authorities commenced a criminal investigation against the individual (tax evasion and fraud). There were civil proceedings in the Czech Courts against the Czech companies relating to disputes over property (which disputes existed before the Claimant bought the shares in those companies).

Complaints had been filed before Czech Courts and the ECHR by the Czech companies, claiming, inter alia, a violation of Article 6 ECHR. The Courts had been asked to grant interim measures by way of release of assets which had been frozen (possible proceeds of crime), but had declined to do so. All in all, a complex context for an ICSID Tribunal to consider preliminary measures.

Additional Considerations

By letter dated 25 January 2007, the Claimant sought provisional measures invoking ICSID Rule 39, and sought transfer of frozen funds to a bank account in favour of the one of the Czech companies. The request for provisional measures was subsequently expanded to include notifications relating to disputed property, and an order seeking examination of Czech Government archives on the (unsubstantiated) grounds that one of the parties in the civil litigation against the Czech companies was *"acting on behalf and with the help of the Czech Government"*.

The Tribunal observed that provisional measures should only be granted in situations of *"absolute necessity and urgency, in order to protect rights that could, absent these measures, be definitely lost"* (para 32). ICJ case law identified the test as being actions *"capable of causing or of threatening irreparable prejudice to the rights invoked"* (*Greece v. Turkey* 1976/page 15). The rights must "exist at the time of the request and not be hypothetical or to be created in the future" (*Maffezini v. Spain* (28/10/1999) (Procedural Order No.2)).

49

The Tribunal declined to order that the Czech authorities should enter a note on the file that certain plots of land should not be sold – because this pre-supposed that there was an ownership right in existence- the very matter subject to dispute before the Czech Courts. The Tribunal noted that Interim Measures are meant to preserve the "status quo" and not improve a party's position.

Likewise the claim for release of frozen funds. As for access to Government archives, the request was a "fishing expedition" (para 43). Hence all requests for interim measures were rejected, in a decision published almost 4 months after the request was first made.

City Oriente Limited v. La República del Ecuador y Empresa Estatal de Petroleos del Ecuador (Petroecuador), ICSID Case No. ARB/06/21 (Decision on Provisional Measures, 19 November 2007)

On 19 November 2007, the Arbitral Tribunal had ordered very wide ranging provisional measures which called upon the Ecuadorian authorities, inter-alia, to refrain from instituting or prosecuting any proceedings or actions of whatsoever nature against the Claimant and its employees arising out of a Contract and/or the effects of the application of a Law seeking amendments in the Hydrocarbons sector.

City Oriente contended that additional monies were being demanded pursuant to the Law which were unjustified vis the Contract, and violated Investor protection rights. On 17 October 2007, a criminal case was initiated in Ecuador against the Claimant's executives – embezzlement – the failure to pay the monies that had been sought. This led to the provisional measures request- granted less than 4 weeks later.

The Claimant contended that there had been a violation of the provisional measures. The Respondent (which had not entered an appearance earlier) applied on 1 February 2008 for the measures to be set aside.

The Tribunal observed that there was no requirement for *"irreparable harm"* – Rule 39 imposed an *"urgency"* requirement.

The Tribunal stated that the *"harm spared to [the Claimant] by such measures must be significant and [must] exceed greatly the damage caused to the party affected thereby"* (para 72) – this looks somewhat like the English Law *American Cyanimid* [1975] AC 396 (HL) *"balance of convenience"* test for interim-injunctive relief.

The Tribunal emphasised that it was not seeking to usurp the sovereign powers of Ecuador, but that the absence of the provisional measures carried a high risk that the Contract would be terminated by the State, in addition to which monies would be demanded from the Claimant which might not be payable or capable of payment- jeopardizing the Claimant's economic feasibility. An eventual award in the ICSID proceedings in favour of the Claimant would not be able to address this adequately. In contrast, the Tribunal considered that if the final award was in favour of the Respondent, it would be compensated for delayed payment by way of interest.

Additional
Considerations

The Tribunal stressed that it was not seeking to prejudge the merits, simply seeking to maintain the status quo pending determination of the Claimant's claim.

Perenco Ecuador Ltd. v. The Republic of Ecuador and Empresa Estatal Petróleos del Ecuador (Petroecuador), ICSID Case No. ARB/08/6 (Decision on Provisional Measures, 8 May 2009)

This ICSID Tribunal was presided over by the late Lord Bingham, in one of the very few arbitration matters he dealt with before his untimely death. There is little doubt (in the author's mind) that the presence of Lord Bingham on the Tribunal led to an order for provisional measures with a significant difference – payment of sums into an escrow account by the Claimant by way of security, in the event that the Claimant did not succeed on the jurisdictional or merits issues.

A request for arbitration had been filed on 30 April 2008. The dispute concerned Participation Contracts for Exploration and Exploitation of Hydrocarbons, conferring an entitlement to engage in oil exploration and production activities.

In April 2006, a new Law was enacted in Ecuador, which the Claimant contended provided for additional payment to the Ecuador authorities in a manner not reflected in the Contracts. The Claimant made the payments sought under protest until April 2008, at which point negotiations for a compromise broke down. In February 2009, enforcement notices were issued against the Claimant for non-payment totaling around US$330 million. On 3 March 2009, the seizure of property belonging to the Claimant was ordered.

In the request for arbitration, the Claimant had sought provisional measures including restraint of the Respondent from collecting the monies purportedly due pursuant to the new Law. During the first ICSID hearing on 7 February 2009 (9 months after the request was filed), Claimant's Counsel stated that he did not intend to pursue the provisional measures request at that juncture.

However, by letter dated 18 February 2009, the request for provisional measures was formally revived.

The Tribunal proceeded on the basis that it had to be satisfied that a prima facie basis for jurisdiction existed (para. 39). In the face of what it considered to be the threat or likelihood of imminent seizure of the Claimant's assets in the sum of around US$330 million, the Tribunal granted the measures sought.

The Respondent retorted that the Tribunal merely had the power to make recommendations and not orders – unsurprisingly, the Tribunal rejected this contention. By way of analogy, the ICJ has a power to *"indicate"* provisional measures which have consistently held to be obligatory in character pursuant to Article 41 of the ICJ's Statute (paras. 68 to 70 - see the discussion thereafter with reference to other International Tribunals, as well as the first ICSID provisional measures decision – *Maffezini* (1999)).

Another case concerning similar circumstances is *Burlington Resources Inc. v. Republic of Ecuador*, ICSID Case No. ARB/08/5 - Request for Arbitration dated 21 April 2008/Provisional

Measures sought on 20 February 2009/order made on 29 June 2009. However, in this case it was also held that an order for provisional remedies only created procedural rights during the currency of the arbitration and that it could not be assimilated to a court's decision to annul a final award (para. 481.)

Quiborax S.A., Non Metallic Minerals S.A. and Allan Fosk Kaplún v. Plurinational State of Bolivia, ICSID Case No. ARB/06/2 (Decision on Provisional Measures, 26 February 2010)

The Tribunal ordered provisional measures by a decision dated 26 February 2010, in response to a request dated 14 September 2009.

The dispute arose from the revocation by Presidential Decree dated 23 June 2004 of eleven mining concessions held by the Claimants in Bolivia. The Claimant contended that the State had engaged in confiscation/expropriation. After the revocation, lengthy negotiations took place which had apparently led to an orally agreed compromise.

Additional Considerations

However, in late 2008, Bolivia initiated criminal proceedings against various persons connected to the Claimant (on the basis that forged corporate documents were being used to support the Claimant's ownership of shares in the original concession holder), leading the Claimant to submit that Bolivia had repudiated the oral settlement agreement.

Bolivian authorities seized documents and questioned various individuals, leading to formal charges being laid against 5 individuals on 16 March 2009. One of the individuals "confessed" to using forged documents to assert entitlements which underpinned the ICSID claim. He was sentenced in August 2009, and immediately pardoned.

The Claimant contended that the criminal proceedings were intended to frustrate the ICSID claim, and in essence asserted that the ICSID claim was being presented upon a false basis. The Claimant argued that the provisional measures were necessary to preserve the status quo, as well as the right of the procedural integrity of the ICSID proceedings.

The Tribunal considered that Bolivia had initiated a corporate audit which had targeted the Claimant because it had initiated the ICSID arbitration (para. 121). Indeed, the Bolivian authorities asserted that the alleged irregularities had only come to light because of the ICSID arbitration.

The Tribunal noted that the Claimant no longer had business operations or a presence in Bolivia. The only co-Claimant who had been implicated in criminal proceedings had not yet been charged and lived outside Bolivia.

Whilst the existence of the criminal proceedings by themselves was of itself objectionable, the fact that potential witnesses might be unwilling to come forward was significant, given that the ICSID proceedings had been characterized in Bolivia as based upon criminal conduct. As a result, the criminal proceedings were considered by the Tribunal to pose a threat to the integrity of the ICSID proceedings.

Accordingly, the Tribunal granted provisional measures requiring Bolivia to suspend criminal proceedings directly related to the arbitration.

For a further illustration of the potential scope for provisional measures see the PCA Tribunal's decision in the case of *Chevron v. Ecuador* [14/5/2010] (PCA Case No. 2009-23). The Notice of Arbitration was served on 23 September 2009 and a request for interim measures made (by email) on 1 April 2010. A hearing took place on 10 and 11 May 2010, leading to the order for Provisional Measures stated to be effective until the next procedural hearing in November 2010.

The order included provision *"not to exert .. pressure on the Court addressing pending litigation in Ecuador"*.. and for the Respondent to *"facilitate.. not discourage, by every appropriate means, the Claimant's engagement of legal experts, advisers .. from the Ecuadorian legal profession for the purpose of these arbitration proceedings (at the Claimants' own expense)."*

PNG Sustainable Development Program Ltd. v. Independent State of Papua New Guinea (ICSID Case No. ARB/13/33) (Decision on the Claimant's Request for Provisional Measures, 21 January 2015))

The Tribunal in this case discussed the level of harm that was required in order to satisfy the requirements for provisional measures.

It is noted (by reference to previous decisions) the variations in approach or the precise wording used by the ICSID tribunals as to whether the requirement is that of "irreparable" harm, or whether a demonstration of "serious" harm will suffice. In the Tribunal's view, "the term "irreparable" harm is properly understood as requiring a showing of a material risk of serious or grave damage to the requesting party, and not harm that is literally "irreparable" in what is sometimes regarded as the narrow common law sense of the term. The degree of "gravity" or "seriousness" of harm that is necessary for an order of provisional relief cannot be specified with precision, and depends in part on the circumstances of the case, the nature of the relief requested and the relative harm to be suffered by each party; suffice it to say that substantial, serious harm, even if not irreparable, is generally sufficient to satisfy this element of the standard for granting provisional measures."

Additional Considerations

The Tribunal stated that it was not necessary that the requesting party prove that *"serious"* harm is certain to occur, but it was instead sufficient to show that there is a material risk that "serious harm" will occur.

As for the requirement of *"urgency"*, the Tribunal's view that was that a request for provisional measures would satisfy the requirement of urgency where it entails *"a question [that] cannot await the outcome of the award on the merits."* The mere passage of time between the Request for Arbitration and the Request for Provisional Measures will not per se be conclusive that there is no urgency.

EuroGas Inc. and Belmont Resources Inc. v. Slovak Republic (ICSID Case No. ARB/14/14) (Decision on Provisional Measures, 23 June 2015)

In this case, both the Claimants and Respondent sought provisional measures.

At the outset, the Tribunal addressed the Respondent's challenge on the grounds of jurisdiction, noting that in an application for provisional measures, the Tribunal needs only to be prima facie satisfied that it has jurisdiction over the dispute. In the instant case, the facts alleged by the Claimants established *"at first sight"* the jurisdiction of the Tribunal and it was not necessary, at this stage, to verify them in depth as the objections raised by the Respondent against the Tribunal's jurisdiction would be fully addressed at a later stage of the proceedings. For the time being, the Tribunal was of the view that the lack of jurisdiction alleged by the Respondent was *"not blatant"*.

In rejecting the Claimants' application, the Tribunal stressed that *"a particularly high threshold"* must be reached before an ICSID tribunal can order provisional measures which interfere with criminal proceedings, as the right and the responsibility to conduct such proceedings is a prerogative of any sovereign State. Further, as the tribunal held in Procedural Order No. 14 in *Churchill Mining*: *"An allegation that the status quo has been altered or that the dispute has been aggravated needs to be buttressed by concrete instances of intimidation or harassment"*.

In rejecting the Respondent's request for security for costs, the Tribunal emphasized the high threshold to be applied and stressed that *RSM v Saint Lucia* was an exceptional case.

Security for Costs

RSM Production Corporation v. Saint Lucia, ICSID Case No. ARB/12/10, Decision on the Respondent's Request for Security for Costs, 13 August 2014

It is highly unusual for an ICSID Tribunal to grant security for costs, although not unheard of. In *RSM Production Corporation v. Saint Lucia*, security for costs was ordered based on the exceptional circumstances of the case (including that the claimant was not only impecunious and funded by a third party, but also had a proven history of not complying with cost orders). Notably, the (majority) decision of the Tribunal (presided over by Prof. Siegfred H Elsing) was handed down alongside assenting reasons from arbitrator Gavan Griffith QC and a dissent from Judge Edward W Nottingham.

The dispute arose in respect of an oil exploration license granted to the Claimant by the Respondent. The Claimant filed a request for arbitration on 2 April 2012. In a letter dated 6 June 2014, the Respondent sought an order obliging the Claimant to post security for costs in addition to its request to order that the Claimant bear all outstanding advances dealt with in the Tribunal's previous decision.

Additional Considerations

The decision observed that although a large number of ICSID tribunals had ruled that a measure requesting the lodging of security for costs does, generally, not fall outside an ICSID tribunal's power provided exceptional circumstances exist, no ICSID ruling had been submitted to the tribunal in which such exceptional circumstances had been established.

The majority noted that contrary to the position in *Maffezini*, which took the view that only *"rights in dispute"* (ie, directly relating to the subject matter of the dispute) could be protected by provisional measures, procedural rights, such as the potential right to obtain reimbursement of costs, could also be protected. Future and conditional rights (such as the potential claim for cost reimbursement) also qualified as *"rights to be preserved"*.

Contrary to the situation in previous ICSID cases where tribunals had declined applications for security for costs because there was no evidence concerning the financial situation of the opposing party, it had been established to the majority of the Tribunal's satisfaction that the Claimant did not have sufficient financial resources. While it had previously been held that such financial limitations did not provide a sufficient basis for ordering security for costs, the Claimant's consistent failures to satisfy previous orders in other ICSID and non-ICSID proceedings provided compelling grounds for granting the Respondent's request.

The presence of third party funding further supported the majority of the Tribunal's position since, in the absence of security or guarantees being offered, it was doubtful as to whether the third party would assume responsibility for honouring an award.

In his assenting reasons, Dr Gavan Griffith QC, while agreeing with the result on the basis of the exceptional circumstances set out in the decision, stated that his preferred ground for making the order concerned the third party funding issue.

Judge Edward Nottingham based his dissent on two grounds:

- First, that he did not think an order requiring the Claimant to secure costs which may be awarded to the Respondent was encompassed in the class of *"provisional measures"* which may *"be taken to preserve the rights"* of the Respondent.

- Second, that entry of an "order" flew in the face of the explicit direction in both Article 47 and Rule 39 that a tribunal may "recommend" provisional measures.

Abuse of process

Europe Cement Investment & Trade S.A. v. Republic of Turkey, ICSID Case No. ARB(AF)/07/2 (Award, 13 August 2009) and Cementownia "Nowa Huta" S.A. v. Republic of Turkey, ICSID Case No. ARB(AF)/06/2 (Award, 17 September 2009)

Both cases concerned claims relating to alleged ownership of shares in companies in Turkey which were engaged in electricity transmission. It was alleged that Turkish legislation in February 2001 had the effect of preventing the Turkish companies from continuing business, as a new State owned entity was established for such purposes.

The issue for consideration in the above cases was whether the Claimant's had established that they were "*investors*" in the Turkish companies – did they own shares?

In both cases there appears to have been a somewhat troublesome procedural process, with Claimant's Counsel coming off the record and numerous procedural orders having been made, for, inter-alia, production of originals of share certificate, but not complied with by the Claimants.

As to the central question, both Tribunals held that proof of ownership of shares in the Turkish companies had not been established, and thus the Claimants were not investors – no jurisdiction.

However, the Tribunals went further and concluded that the Claimants had used forged documents to try to advance fraudulent claims (para. 159, Cementownia - the Europe Cement Tribunal adopted slightly gentler terminology with the same meaning at para 175).

Additional Considerations

The Tribunals both considered whether an award of "moral damages" could be made against the Claimants – and decided against. In the case of *Desert Line Projects LLC v. The Republic of Yemen*, ICSID Case No. ARB/05/17 (Award, 6 February 2008), the Tribunal had awarded the Claimant an amount of US$1 million for "*in particular the physical duress exerted on the Claimant's executives*". Both Tribunals concluded that such an award was only to be made in exceptional circumstances where the harm could be shown.

The Tribunals therefore declined to award any "moral damages" to Turkey, instead awarding all costs claimed (USD$ 4 million and USD$ 5 million respectively) – even though neither Claimant appeared to have any assets (Cementownia had advanced a USD$ 6.4 billion dollar claim- on the basis of having purchased shares in the Turkish companies for around USD$ 50,000. Moreover, Cementownia had sold off all its assets and gone out of business by the time the Tribunal made the costs Award- para 158).

Renée Rose Levy de Levi and Gremcitel v. Republic of Peru, ICSID Case No. ARB/10/17

In the above case, the Tribunal, in a decision dated 9 January 2015, found that a transfer of shares in the Claimant company represented an abuse of process in all the circumstances and warranted an award of costs.

The dispute related to three parcels of land (called "La Herradura", "Punta del Sol", and "La Chira"), located along Peru's Pacific Coast near Lima, within the Municipality of Chorrillos.

During 1995, Gremco, a Peruvian company belonging to the Levy Group, acquired the three parcels of land, which were subsequently transferred to the Peruvian company Gremcitel, one of the two Claimants in this arbitration.

Disputes subsequently arose between the parties, with the Claimants alleging that actions taken by the Respondent in 2007 rendered the Claimants' ownership of the property and associated projects "meaningless".

On 17 May 2011, the Claimants filed a Request for Arbitration with ICSID, alleging breach of the fair and equitable standard set out in the bilateral investment treaty between France and Peru. The Claimants claimed that they fulfilled the nationality requirements set forth in Articles 25 of the ICSID Convention and 1 of the BIT on the basis that Ms. Levy held French nationality (and did not hold Peruvian nationality), and had owned and controlled Gremcitel, a Peruvian company, indirectly since 2005 and directly since 2007.

The Respondent disputed that the Claimants qualified as investors for the purposes of the BIT and the ICSID convention, alleging that the hurried transfer of shares which allegedly made Ms. Levy the controlling shareholder of Gremcitel constitutes an "abuse of process", having been carried out for the sole purpose of attracting the France-Peru BIT protection at a time the dispute had either already arisen or was at least entirely foreseeable.

The Tribunal (comprising Prof. Gabrielle Kaufmann-Kohler as President, with Dr. Eduardo Zuleta and Prof. Raúl E. Vinuesa) held that it was precluded from exercising jurisdiction over the dispute.

In particular, the Tribunal held that the transfer of shares to Ms. Levy had been carried out in order to access the ICSID arbitration process and, on the facts of the present case, thus constituted an abuse of process:

1. Having considered existing arbitral authorities on abuse of process (including *Phoenix Action Ltd. v. The Czech Republic*, ICSID Case No. ARB/06/5 and *Tidewater et al. v. Bolivarian Republic of Venezuela*, ICSID Case No ARB/10/5), the Tribunal noted that a restructuring carried out with the intention to invoke the treaty's protections at a time when the dispute is foreseeable may constitute an abuse of process depending on the circumstances.

   Additional
   Considerations

2. The threshold for a finding of abuse of process was high, as a court or tribunal would obviously not presume an abuse, and would affirm the evidence of an abuse only "*in very exceptional circumstances*".

3. In the current case, that threshold was satisfied. The Tribunal did "*not see how transferring shares to a family member with a foreign nationality would internationalize the project. What was sought to be internationalized was the soon-to-be-crystallized domestic dispute. In other words, the only purpose of the transfer was to obtain access to ICSID/BIT arbitration, which was otherwise precluded.*"

In respect of costs, the Tribunal was of the view that a finding of abuse of process justified an award of costs, and accordingly ordered that the Claimants pay for the entirety of the costs of the proceedings against the unsuccessful party and also make a contribution to the legal costs of the Respondent.

The Claimants were not ordered to pay the full legal costs of the Respondent, on the basis that while the Claimants sought to minimize the costs of the proceedings, the Respondent had not (which was evidenced by the disparity of the costs figures).

Illegality

SAUR International SA v. Republic of Argentina (ICSID Case No. ARB/04/4) (Decision on Jurisdiction and Liability)

The applicable Argentina-France BIT did not contain an explicit requirement that investments be made in accordance with the legislation of the host State. The tribunal held, however, that the principle of legality and good faith exists regardless of whether the treaty expresses it in explicit terms. In the tribunal's view, this principle would preclude investors who engage in "serious violation of the legal order" of the host State from benefitting from treaty protection (para. 308).

Previously, questions of illegality had been considered as only in terms of their explicit incorporation into the relevant BIT.

Third party funding

Third party funding is becoming more prevalent in arbitration, including investment treaty arbitration. It raises a number of issues, including disclosure obligations (both in relation to the claimant (who is normally the funded party) and the arbitrators) and the impact of third party funding on the conduct of the arbitration/preliminary measures.[2] Certain of these issues were outlined briefly in the ICC Commission Report "Decisions on Costs in International Arbitration"

---

[2] Note, in contrast, the approach taken by some national courts. In *Excalibur Ventures LLC v Texas Keystone Inc* [2014] EWHC 3436 (Comm), the English High Court held that the funding of hopeless and speculative litigation was in itself grounds for a costs order on the indemnity basis. The Judge ordered that each of the litigation funders in that case was to be liable for their contributions to the funding in addition to their contributions provided for security for costs. Liability was assessed from the date that each had begun to provide funding. There is an appeal outstanding against this decision.

(approved by the Commission on Arbitration and ADR at its meeting in Paris on 7 May 2015 and by the ICC Executive Board at its 149th Session in New Delhi on 16 September 2015) which considered disclosure, interim and conservatory measures, and the recoverability of costs.

In *Alemanni v The Argentine Republic, ICSID Case No. ARB/07/8*, the Tribunal observed, *"the Tribunal feels bound to make mention of some aspects of the arrangements for the representation of the Claimants in these proceedings. The Tribunal does not accept the full range of the criticisms made by the Respondent in this regard, since many of the aspects criticised are merely characteristic of the incidents of third-party funding in international investment arbitration. Individual views may differ as to whether third-party funding is or is not desirable or beneficial, either at the national or at the international level, but the practice is by now so well established both within many national jurisdictions and within international investment arbitration that it offers no grounds in itself for objection to the admissibility of a request to arbitrate"*. The Tribunal in that case raised concerns because the claimants had not only signed away their right to obtain more than a percentage of the pro rata outcome of an eventual Award in their favour, but in addition abandoned any right of control over the conduct of the arbitration (including the potential settlement of their claims) and had given a power of attorney to an individual who had not appeared before the Tribunal (the arbitration had been conduct solely by counsel).

Additional Considerations

Impact on arbitral proceedings

Ioannis Kardassopoulos and Ron Fuchs v Georgia

In *Kardassopoulos and Fuchs v Georgia* (ICSID Case No. ARB/07/16), the Claimants, having been successful on jurisdiction and liability, applied for their costs. The Respondent objected inter alia on the basis that the Claimants' costs were in fact borne by third-party funding and thus there was an arguable case that the Claimants' costs were not recoverable.

By an Award dated 3 March 2010, the Tribunal (L. Yves Fortier QC (President), Professor Francisco Orrego Vicuna and Professor Vaughan Lowe QC) held that it *"knows of no principle why any such third party financing arrangement should be taken into consideration in determining the amount of recovery by the Claimants of their costs"*.

Furthermore, Georgia had Bilateral Investment Treaties with Greece and Israel, both of which provided that a Contracting Party was precluded from filing any objection to the other party receiving *"compensation or an indemnity under an insurance contract in respect of all or part of the damages incurred"*. Third-party funding was not inherently different from an insurance arrangement.

The Respondent was ordered to pay the Claimants' costs.

RSM Production Corporation v. Saint Lucia, ICSID Case No. ARB/12/10 (Decision on the Respondent's Request for Security for Costs, 13 August 2014)

In *RSM Production Corporation v. Saint Lucia*, one of the key factors for the majority of the tribunal which ordered security for costs was the existence of third party funding.

In his assenting reasons, Dr Gavan Griffith QC, while agreeing with the result on the basis of the exceptional circumstances set out in the decision, stated that his preferred ground for making the order concerned the third party funding issue. In particular, he noted:

1. It is increasingly common for BIT claims to be financed by an identified or (as here) unidentified third party funder.

2. This could not have been foreseen by the founders of the ICSID Convention. *"In this regard, the integrity of the BIT Regimes is apt to be recalibrated in the case of a third party funder, related or unrelated, to mandate that its real exposure to costs orders which may go one way to it on success should flow the other direction on failure."*

3. Unless there are particular reasons militating to the contrary, exceptional circus manes may be found to justify security of costs orders arising under BIT claims as against a third party funder, related or unrelated, which does not proffer adequate security for adverse costs orders. An example of contrary circumstances might be to establish that the funded claimant has independent capacity to meet costs orders.

4. Once it appears that there is third party funding of an investor's claims, the onus is cast on the claimant to disclose all relevant factors and to make a case why security for costs orders should not be made.

Judge Edward Nottingham dissented from the majority's decision. In relation to third party funding, Judge Nottingham suggested various potential issues – whether it should be permitted and under what conditions; that information about that nature of the funding or the identity of the funder should be relevant; the terms of the funding contract; how third party funding was defined and whether it could include an insurance contrary under which a State financed its defense - but said that those could and should be addressed by the Administrative Council in its rule making capacity if there was a problem, and not by individual tribunals.

Additional Considerations

EuroGas Inc. and Belmont Resources Inc. v. Slovak Republic (ICSID Case No. ARB/14/14) (Decision on Provisional Measures, 23 June 2015)

In *EuroGas Inc. v Slovak Republic*, the Tribunal distinguished the decision in *RSM Production Corporation v. Saint Lucia*. Although the claimant was third party funded in *EuroGas*, no order for security for costs was made as the exceptional circumstances which existed in *RSM v St Lucia* were not made out in the present case.

Disclosure

In *Muhammet Cap & Sehil Inşaat Endustri ve Ticaret Ltd Sti v Turkmenistan (Sehil), ICSID Case No. ARB/12/6*, an ICSID Tribunal considered claims brought by Turkish investors related to the alleged destruction, impairment and unlawful expropriation of construction projects in Turkmenistan.

On 11 April 2014, the Respondent invited the Tribunal (Professor Julian Lew QC (President), Professor Laurence Boisson de Chazournes and Professor Bernard Hanotiau) to order the Claimants to disclose:

1. whether they had entered into third-party funding arrangements to finance their claims;

2. if so, the terms of those arrangements; and

3. the existence of contingency fee arrangements with either the Claimants' counsel or third-party funders.

By Procedural Order No.2 dated 23 June 2014, the Tribunal held that *"it has inherent powers to make orders of the nature requested where necessary to preserve the rights of the parties and the integrity of the process"*.

In light of the fact that none of the parties had suggested any factors to be taken into account for the consideration of the request for disclosure, the Tribunal deemed the following factors to be relevant to justify an order for disclosure of details of third-party funding arrangements:

1. To avoid a conflict of interest for the arbitrator as a result of the third-party funder;

2. For transparency and to identify the true party to the case;

3. For the Tribunal to fairly decide how costs should be allocated at the end of any arbitration;

4. If there is an application for security for costs if requested; and

5. To ensure that confidential information which may come out during the arbitral proceedings is not disclosed to parties with ulterior motives.

Procedural Order No.2 rejected the application for disclosure, but stated that the Respondent was not precluded from making further applications.

By Procedural Order No.3 dated 12 June 2015, on a further application for disclosure of third-party funding arrangements, the Tribunal ordered the Claimants to disclose within 15 days from the date of the order the identity and nature of the involvement of third-party funders due to the following:

1. it was necessary to ensure the integrity of the arbitral process and to determine whether any of the arbitrators were affected by the presence of the third-party funder;

2. the Respondent had indicated (though had not yet brought) an application for security for costs;

3. there had been no denial from the Claimants that third-party funders were involved;

4. the Respondent had still not been paid a costs order in her favour in another arbitral matter (*Kiliç İnşaat İthalat İhracat Sanayi ve Ticaret Anonim Şirketi, ICSID Case No. ARB/10/1*) even though that claimant had funded annulment proceedings. There was a danger that the Claimants would be unable to meet a costs order in the instant arbitration *"and the third-party funder will have disappeared as it is not a party to this arbitration"*.

ROLE OF NATIONAL COURTS

Where an investment dispute arises, often a claimant will prefer not to go to the local courts for resolution of an issue (except insofar as it is required by a bilateral investment treaty) but will instead seek recourse in investment arbitration proceedings. There is a (not necessarily unfounded concern) that given the large sums of money and potential national interests, national courts may not provide an entirely impartial and neutral forum.

Nonetheless, national courts may have a role to play both during the arbitration proceedings, and after.

Supporting investment treaty arbitration proceedings

The availability of interim/provisional measures in investment treaty arbitration proceedings depends in part on the applicable arbitration rules.

Previously, there was some confusion as to whether a national court could order measures in support of ICSID arbitration, with contradictory decisions being issued by both national courts and ICSID tribunals.[3] The amendments made in 1984 to the ICSID Arbitration Rules included the addition of an explicit provision on interim measures (now Rule 3(6)), providing *"Nothing in this Rule shall prevent the parties, provided that they have so stipulated in the agreement recording their consent, from requesting any judicial or other authority to order provisional measures, prior to or after the institution of the proceeding, for the preservation of their respective rights and interests."*[4]

Rule 39 was considered in the English Court of Appeal case of *ETI Euro Telecom International NV v Bolivia [2008] EWCA Civ*

---

[3] Article 47 of the ICSID Convention reads, *"Except as the parties otherwise agree, the Tribunal may, if it considers that the circumstances so require, recommend any provisional measures which should be taken to preserve the respective rights of either party."*
[4] In contrast, Article 26(9) of the UNCITRAL Arbitration Rules (as amended in 2010) makes provision for a party to seek interim measures from a national court.

880. The claimant, a Netherlands company, had commenced ICSID arbitration proceedings against Bolivia in respect of the nationalization of a subsidiary company, in which Bolivia did not participate. The claimant subsequently obtained an ex parte order of attachment in New York in aid of the ICSID arbitration in respect of certain bank deposits held in New York in the subsidiary company's name, and then obtained, before the English courts, a freezing order (without notice) in respect of about US$50 million held on deposit in London in the same subsidiary company's name pursuant to section 25 of the Civil Jurisdiction and Judgments Act 1982.

Following discharge of the freezing order at first instance, the claimant appealed to the Court of Appeal.

The Court of Appeal dismissed the appeal. Section 25 required the foreign proceedings in which an order was made in support of to be proceedings on the substantive issues. In the present case, the substantive issues were being dealt with in arbitration and not in the New York proceedings. Furthermore, the arbitration proceedings could not be "proceedings" within the meaning of section 25:

1. The Arbitration Act 1996 dealt with interim injunctions in respect of ICSID proceedings; not the Civil Jurisdiction and Judgments Act 1982. Under the 1996 Act, the Lord Chancellor had the power to direct by order that (inter alia) section 44 of the Arbitration Act 1996 should apply to ICSID arbitrations. No such order had been made.

2. The fact that the power to extend section 44 to ICSID arbitrations exists indicates, if anything, that the power does not exist elsewhere. It has not been exercised because there is no need for such a power in the light of Article 26 of the ICSID Convention and Rule 39(6) of the Arbitration Rules

Enforcement of Investment Arbitration Awards

Enforcement of an investment arbitration award differs depending on the arbitration rules involved:

ICSID

Article 54 of the ICSID Convention provides that *"Each Contracting State shall recognize an award rendered pursuant to this Convention as binding and enforce the pecuniary obligations imposed by that award within its territories as if it were a final judgment of a court in that State."* In order to enforce an award, a party must provide to the competent authority or court a copy of the award certified by the Secretary-General.

An award made by an ICSID Tribunal shall (pursuant to Article 53) is binding on the parties and not subject to any appeal or to any other remedy except those provided for in this Convention. Accordingly, there is no basis on which national courts can conduct their own review of the award on the basis of error of law or fact, or refuse to enforce on grounds of public policy. This restriction is qualified only by Article 55, which states that Article 54 is not to be construed as derogating from the law in force in any Contracting State relating to sovereign immunity.

UNCITRAL Rules

As explained further below, in contrast to the position under ICSID (in England and Wales), no specific legislative regime applies where an award has been handed down pursuant to the UNCITRAL rules – instead, enforcement falls under the general provisions for enforcement of arbitration awards (as set out in the Arbitration Act 1996, the precise regime depending on whether the seat of the arbitration was England, a New York Convention state, or otherwise).

England and Wales

The Arbitration Act 1996 sets out the provision for the enforcement of arbitration awards with their seat in England (section 66) or a New York Convention state (sections 100-103). Such awards are open to challenge on the limited grounds set out in the applicable sections of that Act.

A special scheme exists in respect of ICSID arbitration awards, being the Arbitration (International Investment Disputes) Act 1966 which makes provision for the recognition and enforcement of awards rendered pursuant to the ICSID Convention. Pursuant to section 1, a person seeking recognition or enforcement of an ICSID award shall be entitled to have the award registered in the High Court – the effect of registration being to make the award of the same force and effect for the purposes of execution as if it had been a judgment of the High Court (section 2).

While the majority of challenges before the English courts have been in respect of contractual arbitrations, the courts have considered challenges in the context of investment treaty arbitration.

Ecuador v Occidental Exploration & Production Co [2006] 2 W.L.R. 70

In *Ecuador v Occidental Exploration & Production Co* [2006] 2 W.L.R. 70, the Court of Appeal held that it did have jurisdiction in respect of a challenge to an award made under the UNCITRAL Rules.

By way of background, the appellant, a California corporation, appealed against a decision of the English High Court that the English courts had jurisdiction to entertain an application by the respondent, the Republic of Ecuador, challenging the jurisdiction of an arbitration tribunal. The arbitration had been conducted under UNCITRAL Rules, with the seat of the arbitration being London.

The Court of Appeal held that, as the seat of the arbitration was in London, it did have jurisdiction to entertain challenges to awards based on sections 67 and 68 of the Arbitration Act 1996 (appeals on the substance of such awards could not come before an English court under section 69(1) of the Arbitration

Act 1996 except in so far as they were regarded as raising a question of law within the meaning of that section).

United States

In respect of ICSID arbitration awards, 22 U.S. Code § 1650a (Arbitration awards under the Convention) provides, *"(a)* ***Treaty rights; enforcement; full faith and credit; nonapplication of Federal Arbitration Act****: An award of an arbitral tribunal rendered pursuant to chapter IV of the convention shall create a right arising under a treaty of the United States. The pecuniary obligations imposed by such an award shall be enforced and shall be given the same full faith and credit as if the award were a final judgment of a court of general jurisdiction of one of the several States. The Federal Arbitration Act (9 U.S.C. 1 et seq.) shall not apply to enforcement of awards rendered pursuant to the convention."*

In a paper by the New York City Bar (Committee on International Comercial Disputes) (July 2012), the Committee stated that it was aware of only a handful of cases in the US courts considering the recognition and enforcement of ICSID awards (all of which had been decided by the federal court in the Southern District of New York). In each case, the court recognized and enforced the ICSID award. Those cases included *Liberian Eastern Timber Corp. v. Republic of Liberia*, 650 F. Supp. 73, 75 (S.D.N.Y. 1986); *Enron Corp. v. Argentine Republic*, No. M-82 (S.D.N.Y. Nov. 20, 2007); and *Sempra Energy Int'l v. Argentine Republic*, No. M-82 (S.D.N.Y. Nov. 14, 2007).

In later cases, the US courts have also rejected challenges by losing states to ICSID decisions, including in *Blue Ridge Investments, LLC v Republic of Argentina* (Southern District of New York, 30 September 2012) and *Duke Energy Int'l v Republic of Peru* (DC District Court, 19 November 2012).

The key issue before the US Courts is what form such enforcement proceedings may take, and in particular, whether ex parte proceedings are permissible (with a split currently existing between district courts on this matter).

72

Continental Europe

When considering the enforcement of ICSID awards, recent developments in continental Europe must also be considered, and in particular, the European Commission's actions in respect of the arbitration award handed down in the ICSID case of *Micula & Ors v Romania*, ICSID Case No.ARB/05/20.

In July 2005, the Claimants submitted a request for ICSID arbitration to decide disputes relating to breach of their legitimate expectations that the incentives would run until at least 2009, and violation of the obligation of fair and equitable treatment owed to Swedish investors under the Romania-Sweden Bilateral Investment Treaty ("BIT").

On 19 June 2009, the Commission was given permission to intervene in the arbitration proceedings. The Commission submitted that the incentives were incompatible with the European Union's rule on regional aid and that any ruling by the Tribunal that reinstated those privileges would lead to the granting of new aid which would also be incompatible.

On 11 December 2013, the Tribunal (Dr Laurent Levy, President, Dr Stanimir Alexandrov and Professor Georges Abi-Saab) gave its Award by which it ordered Romania to pay €82 million as damages for its failure to ensure a fair and equitable treatment of the claimants' investments in violating of the Romania-Sweden BIT.

By way of a letter dated 26 May 2014, the European Commission informed Romania of its decision to issue a suspension injunction obliging Romania to suspend any action which may lead to the implementation of the outstanding parts of the Award as such implementation would constitute unlawful State aid.

On 1 October 2014 (as reported in the Official Journal of the European Union), the Commission notified Romania that that a formal investigation would be commenced. Following an investigation, on 20 March 2015, the European Commission concluded that compensation paid by Romania to two Swedish

Role of
National
Courts

investors for an abolished investment aid scheme breaches EU state aid rules and required repayment of the part of the award that Romania had already paid to the claimants.

The claimants have filed a case against the European Commission (Case T-646/14) in respect of this decision. A decision by the General Court will be of great interest (and significance) to claimants and respondent states.[5]

---

[5] Note that proceedings are also underway in the US courts for enforcement of the award, which has been challenged by Romania. The European Commission has been granted permission to file an amicus curiae brief in those proceedings – see the decision of Judge Schofield filed on 5 August 2015 which considered both the enforceability of ICSID awards and the impact of the EC's position.

ANNEX 1: Sample Bilateral Investment Treaty

Agreement Between the Government of Canada and the Government of the People's Republic of China for the Promotion and Reciprocal Protection of Investments

(in force from 1 October 2014)

The Government of Canada and the Government of the People's Republic of China (the "Contracting Parties"),

Recognizing the need to promote investment based on the principles of sustainable development;

Desiring to intensify the economic cooperation of both States, based on equality and mutual benefit;

Have agreed as follows:

Part A

Article 1

Definitions

For the purpose of this Agreement,

1. "investment" means:

(a) an enterprise;

(b) shares, stocks and other forms of equity participation in an enterprise;

(c) bonds, debentures, and other debt instruments of an enterprise;

(d) a loan to an enterprise

(i) where the enterprise is an affiliate of the investor, or

(ii) where the original maturity of the loan is at least three years;

(e) notwithstanding sub-paragraphs (c) and (d) above, a loan to or debt security issued by a financial institution is an investment only where the loan or debt security is treated as regulatory capital by the Contracting Party in whose territory the financial institution is located;

(f) an interest in an enterprise that entitles the owner to share in the income or profits of the enterprise;

(g) an interest in an enterprise that entitles the owner to share in the assets of that enterprise on dissolution;

(h) interests arising from the commitment of capital or other resources in the territory of a Contracting Party to economic activity in such territory, such as under

(i) contracts involving the presence of an investor's property in the territory of the Contracting Party, including turnkey or construction contracts, or concessions to search for and extract oil and other natural resources, or

(ii) contracts where remuneration depends substantially on the production, revenue or profits of an enterprise;

(i) intellectual property rights; and

(j) any other tangible or intangible, moveable or immovable, property and related property rights acquired or used for business purposes;

but "investment" does not mean:

(k) claims to money that arise solely from

(i) commercial contracts for the sale of goods or services, or

(ii) the extension of credit in connection with a commercial transaction, such as trade financing, other than a loan covered by sub-paragraph (d); or

(l) any other claims to money,

that do not involve the kinds of interests set out in sub-paragraphs (a) to (j);

2. "investor" means with regard to either Contracting Party:

(a) any natural person who has the citizenship or status of permanent resident of that Contracting Party in accordance with its laws and who does not possess the citizenship of the other Contracting Party;

(b) any enterprise as defined in paragraph 10(a) of this Article;

that seeks to make, is making or has made a covered investment;

3. "investment of an investor of a Contracting Party" means an investment owned or controlled directly or indirectly by an investor of such Contracting Party;

4. "covered investment" means, with respect to a Contracting Party, an investment in its territory of an investor of the other Contracting Party existing on the date of entry into force of this Agreement or an investment of an investor admitted in accordance with its laws and regulations thereafter, and which involves the commitment of capital or other resources, the expectation of gain or profit, or the assumption of risk;

5. "returns" means the amounts yielded by investments, and in particular, though not limited to, profits, capital gains, dividends, interest, royalties, returns-in-kind or other income;

6. "measure" includes any law, regulation, rule, procedure, decision, requirement, administrative action, or practice;

7. "existing measure" means a measure existing at the time this Agreement enters into force;

8. "financial service" has the same meaning as in sub-paragraph 5(a) of the Annex on Financial Services of the GATS;

9. "financial institution" means any financial intermediary or other enterprise that is authorized to do business and is regulated or supervised as a financial institution under the law of the Contracting Party in whose territory it is located;

10. "enterprise" means:

(a) any entity constituted or organized in accordance with the laws of a Contracting Party, such as public institutions, corporations, foundations, agencies, cooperatives, trust, societies, associations and similar entities and private companies, firms, partnerships, establishments, joint ventures and organizations, whether or not for profit, and irrespective of whether their liabilities are limited or otherwise; and

(b) a branch of any such entity

11. "intellectual property rights" means copyright and related rights, trademark rights, patent rights, rights in layout designs of semiconductor integrated circuits, trade secret rights, plant breeders' rights, rights in geographical indications and industrial design rights;

12. "confidential information" means business confidential information and information that is privileged or otherwise protected from disclosure;

13. "disputing investor" means an investor that makes a claim under Article 20;

14. "disputing Contracting Party" means a Contracting Party against which a claim is made under Article 20;

15. "disputing party" means the disputing investor or the disputing Contracting Party;

16. "ICSID" means the International Centre for Settlement of Investment Disputes;

17. "ICSID Convention" means the Convention on the Settlement of Investment Disputes between States and Nationals of other States, done at Washington on 18 March 1965;

18. "Additional Facility Rules of ICSID" means the Rules Governing the Additional Facility for the Administration of Proceedings by the Secretariat of the International Centre for Settlement of Investment Disputes and Schedule C (Arbitration) thereto, approved by the Administrative Council on 29 September 2002, as amended from time to time;

19. "Tribunal" means an arbitration tribunal established under Part C;

20. "UNCITRAL Arbitration Rules" means the Arbitration Rules of the United Nations Commission on International

Trade Law, approved by the United Nations General Assembly on 15 December 1976, as amended from time to time;

21. "WTO Agreement" means the Agreement Establishing the World Trade Organization done at Marrakesh on 15 April 1994;

22. "territory" means:

In respect of Canada:

(a) the land territory, air space, internal waters and territorial sea over which Canada exercises sovereignty;

(b) the exclusive economic zone of Canada, as determined by its domestic law pursuant to Part V of the United Nations Convention on the Law of the Sea (UNCLOS); and

(c) the continental shelf of Canada as determined by its domestic law pursuant to Part VI UNCLOS.

In respect of China:

the territory of China, including land territory, internal waters, territorial sea, territorial air space, and any maritime areas beyond the territorial sea over which, in accordance with international law and its domestic law, China exercises sovereign rights or jurisdiction with respect to the waters, seabed and subsoil and natural resources thereof.

Part B

Article 2

Scope and Application

1. This Agreement shall apply to measures adopted or maintained by a Contracting Party relating to investors of the other Contracting Party and covered investments.

2. A Contracting Party's obligations under this Agreement shall apply to any entity whenever that entity exercises any regulatory, administrative or other governmental authority delegated to it by that Contracting Party, such as the power to

expropriate, grant licenses, approve commercial transactions or impose quotas, fees or other charges.

3. Each Contracting Party shall take all necessary measures in order to ensure observance of the provisions of this Agreement by provincial governments.2

Article 3

Promotion and Admission of Investment

Each Contracting Party shall encourage investors of the other Contracting Party to make investments in its territory and admit such investments in accordance with its laws, regulations and rules.

Article 4

Minimum Standard of Treatment

1. Each Contracting Party shall accord to covered investments fair and equitable treatment and full protection and security, in accordance with international law.

2. The concepts of "fair and equitable treatment" and "full protection and security" in paragraph 1 do not require treatment in addition to or beyond that which is required by the international law minimum standard of treatment of aliens as evidenced by general State practice accepted as law.

3. A determination that there has been a breach of another provision of this Agreement, or of a separate international agreement, does not establish that there has been a breach of this Article.

Article 5

Most-Favoured-Nation Treatment

1. Each Contracting Party shall accord to investors of the other Contracting Party treatment no less favourable than that it accords, in like circumstances, to investors of a non-Contracting Party with respect to the establishment, acquisition, expansion,

management, conduct, operation and sale or other disposition of investments in its territory.

2. Each Contracting Party shall accord to covered investments treatment no less favourable than that it accords, in like circumstances, to investments of investors of a non-Contracting Party with respect to the establishment, acquisition, expansion, management, conduct, operation and sale or other disposition of investments in its territory.

3. For greater certainty, the "treatment" referred to in paragraphs 1 and 2 of this Article does not encompass the dispute resolution mechanisms, such as those in Part C, in other international investment treaties and other trade agreements.

Article 6

National Treatment

1. Each Contracting Party shall accord to investors of the other Contracting Party treatment no less favourable than that it accords, in like circumstances, to its own investors with respect to the expansion, management, conduct, operation and sale or other disposition of investments in its territory.

2. Each Contracting Party shall accord to covered investments treatment no less favourable than that it accords, in like circumstances, to investments of its own investors with respect to the expansion, management, conduct, operation and sale or other disposition of investments in its territory.

3. The concept of "expansion" in this Article applies only with respect to sectors not subject to a prior approval process under the relevant sectoral guidelines and applicable laws, regulations and rules in force at the time of expansion. The expansion may be subject to prescribed formalities and other information requirements.

Article 7

Senior Management, Boards of Directors and Entry of Personnel

1. A Contracting Party may not require that an enterprise of that Party, that is a covered investment, appoint individuals of any particular nationality to senior management positions.

2. A Contracting Party may require that a majority of the board of directors, or any committee thereof, of an enterprise of that Contracting Party that is a covered investment be of a particular nationality or resident in the territory of the Contracting Party, provided that the requirement does not materially impair the ability of the investor to exercise control over its investment.

3. Subject to its laws, regulations and policies relating to the entry and sojourn of non-citizens, a Contracting Party shall permit natural persons who have the citizenship or status of permanent resident of the other Contracting Party and are employed by any enterprise that is a covered investment of an investor, or a subsidiary or affiliate thereof, to enter and remain temporarily in its territory in a capacity that is managerial, executive or that requires specialized knowledge.

Article 8

Exceptions

1. Article 5 does not apply to:

(a) treatment by a Contracting Party pursuant to any existing or future bilateral or multilateral agreement:

(i) establishing, strengthening or expanding a free trade area or customs union; or

(ii) relating to aviation, fisheries, or maritime matters including salvage;

(b) treatment accorded under any bilateral or multilateral international agreement in force prior to 1 January 1994.

2. Articles 5, 6 and 7 do not apply to:

(a)

(i) any existing non-conforming measures maintained within the territory of a Contracting Party; and

(ii) any measure maintained or adopted after the date of entry into force of this Agreement that, at the time of sale or other disposition of a government's equity interests in, or the assets of, an existing state enterprise or an existing governmental entity, prohibits or imposes limitations on the ownership or control of equity interests or assets or imposes nationality requirements relating to senior management or members of the board of directors;

(b) the continuation or prompt renewal of any non-conforming measure referred to in sub-paragraph (a); or

(c) an amendment to any non-conforming measure referred to in sub paragraph (a), to the extent that the amendment does not decrease the conformity of the measure, as it existed immediately before the amendment, with Articles 5, 6 and 7.

3. Articles 5, 6 and 7 do not apply to any measure that a Contracting Party has reserved the right to adopt or maintain pursuant to Annex B.8.

4. In respect of intellectual property rights, a Contracting Party may derogate from Articles 3, 5 and 6 in a manner that is consistent with international agreements regarding intellectual property rights to which both Contracting Parties are parties.

5. Articles 5, 6 and 7, do not apply to:

(a) procurement by a Contracting Party;

(b) subsidies or grants provided by a Contracting Party, including government-supported loans, guarantees and insurance.

Article 9

Performance Requirements

The Contracting Parties reaffirm their obligations under the WTO Agreement on Trade-Related Investment Measures (TRIMs), as amended from time to time. Article 2 and the Annex of the TRIMs are incorporated into and made part of this Agreement.

Article 10

Expropriation

1. Covered investments or returns of investors of either Contracting Party shall not be expropriated, nationalized or subjected to measures having an effect equivalent to expropriation or nationalization in the territory of the other Contracting Party (hereinafter referred to as "expropriation"), except for a public purpose, under domestic due procedures of law, in a non-discriminatory manner and against compensation.6 Such compensation shall amount to the fair market value of the investment expropriated immediately before the expropriation, or before the impending expropriation became public knowledge, whichever is earlier, shall include interest at a normal commercial rate until the date of payment, and shall be effectively realizable, freely transferable, and made without delay. The investor affected shall have a right, under the law of the Contracting Party making the expropriation, to prompt review, by a judicial or other independent authority of that Contracting Party, of his or its case and of the valuation of his or its investment in accordance with the principles set out in this paragraph.

2. This Article does not apply to the issuance of compulsory licenses granted in relation to intellectual property rights, or to other measures in respect of intellectual property rights, to the extent that such measures are consistent with international agreements regarding intellectual property rights to which both Contracting Parties are parties.

Article 11

Compensation for Losses

Investors of one Contracting Party who suffer losses in respect of covered investments owing to war, a state of national emergency, insurrection, riot or other similar events, shall be accorded treatment by the other Contracting Party, in respect of restitution, indemnification, compensation or other settlement, no less favourable than it accords in like circumstances, to its own investors or to investors of any third State.

Article 12

Transfers

1. A Contracting Party shall permit all transfers relating to a covered investment to be made freely and without delay. Such transfers include:

(a) contributions to capital;

(b) profits, capital gains, dividends, interest, royalties including payments in relation to intellectual and industrial property rights, fees, returns-in-kind or other income derived from the investment;

(c) proceeds obtained from the total or partial sale of the covered investment, or from the partial or complete liquidation of the investment;

(d) payments made under a contract entered into by an investor, or its covered investments, including those pursuant to a loan agreement;

(e) payments made pursuant to Articles 10 and 11 and arising under Part C; and

(f) earnings of nationals of a Contracting Party who work in connection with an investment in the territory of the other Contracting Party.

2. Each Contracting Party shall permit transfers relating to a covered investment to be made in a freely convertible currency

at the market rate of exchange prevailing on the date of transfer. In the event that the market rate of exchange does not exist, the rate of exchange shall correspond to the cross rate obtained from those rates which would be applied by the International Monetary Fund on the date of payment for conversions of currencies concerned into Special Drawing Rights.

3. Notwithstanding the provisions of paragraphs 1 and 2 of this Article, a Contracting Party may prevent a transfer through the equitable, non-discriminatory and good faith application of its laws relating to:

(a) bankruptcy, insolvency or the protection of the rights of creditors;

(b) issuing, trading or dealing in securities;

(c) criminal or penal offenses

(d) reports of transfers of currency or other monetary instruments; or

(e) ensuring the satisfaction of judgments in adjudicatory proceedings.

4. (a) Nothing in the Agreement shall be construed to prevent a Contracting Party from adopting or maintaining measures that restrict transfers when the Contracting Party experiences serious balance of payment difficulties, or the threat thereof, provided that such measures:

(i) are of limited duration, applied on a good-faith basis, and should be phased out as the situation calling for imposition of such measures improves;

(ii) do not constitute a dual or multiple exchange rate practice;

(iii) do not otherwise interfere with an investor's ability to invest, in the territory of the Contracting Party, in the form chosen by the investor and, as relevant, in local currency, in any assets that are restricted from being transferred out of the territory of the Contracting Party;

(iv) are applied on an equitable and non-discriminatory basis;

(v) are promptly published by the government authorities responsible for financial services or central bank of the Contracting Party;

(vi) are consistent with the Articles of Agreement of the International Monetary Fund done at Bretton Woods on 22 July 1944; and

(vii) avoid unnecessary damage to the commercial, economic and financial interests of the other Contracting Party.

(b)   Sub-paragraph (a) does not apply to measures that restrict payments or transfers for current transactions8, unless the imposition of such measures complies with the procedures set out in the Articles of Agreement of the International Monetary Fund.

5. Notwithstanding paragraph 1, a Contracting Party may restrict transfers of returns-in-kind in circumstances where it could otherwise restrict such transfers under the WTO Agreement.

Article 13

Subrogation

1. If a Contracting Party or its Agency makes a payment to one of its investors under a guarantee or contract of insurance it has granted to a covered investment of that investor, the other Contracting Party shall recognize the transfer of any right or claim of that investor to the first mentioned Contracting Party or its Agency. The subrogated right or claim shall not be greater than the original right or claim of the said investor. Such right may be exercised by the Contracting Party or any agent thereof so authorized.

2. In an arbitration under Part C, a disputing Contracting Party shall not assert, as a defence, counterclaim, right of setoff or otherwise, that the disputing investor has received or will receive, pursuant to an insurance or guarantee contract, indemnification or other compensation for all or part of its alleged damages.

Article 14

Taxation

1. Except as provided in this Article nothing in this Agreement shall apply to taxation measures.

2. Nothing in this Agreement shall affect the rights and obligations of the Contracting Parties under any tax convention. In the event of any inconsistency between the provisions of this Agreement and any such convention, the provisions of that convention shall apply to the extent of the inconsistency.

3. Nothing in this Agreement shall be construed to require a Contracting Party to furnish or allow access to information the disclosure of which would be contrary to the Contracting Party's law protecting information concerning the taxation affairs of a taxpayer.

4. The provisions of Article 10 shall apply to taxation measures.

5. No claim may be made by an investor pursuant to paragraph 4 unless:

(a) the investor provides a copy of the notice of claim to the taxation authorities of the Contracting Parties; and

(b) six months after receiving notification of the claim by the investor, the taxation authorities of the Contracting Parties fail to reach a joint determination that the measure in question is not an expropriation.

6. The taxation authorities referred to in this Article shall be the following until otherwise notified by a Contracting Party:

(a) for Canada: the Assistant Deputy Minister, Tax Policy, of the Department of Finance Canada;

(b) for China: the Ministry of Finance and State Administration of Taxation or an authorized representative of the Ministry of Finance and State Administration of Taxation.

7. The Contracting Parties shall notify each other promptly by diplomatic note of the successors to the tax authorities identified in sub-paragraphs 6(a) and (b).

Article 15

Disputes between the Contracting Parties

1. Any dispute between the Contracting Parties concerning the interpretation or application of this Agreement shall, as far as possible, be settled by consultation through diplomatic channels.

2. If a dispute cannot thus be settled within six months, it shall, upon the request of either Contracting Party, be submitted to an ad hoc arbitral tribunal.

3. Such tribunal shall be comprised of three arbitrators. Within two months from the date on which either Contracting Party receives the written notice requesting arbitration from the other Contracting Party, each Contracting Party shall appoint one arbitrator. Those two arbitrators shall jointly select a third arbitrator, who shall be a national of a third State which has diplomatic relations with both Contracting Parties. The third arbitrator shall be appointed by the two Contracting Parties as Chairman of the arbitral tribunal within two months from the date of appointment of the other two arbitrators.

4. If within the periods specified in paragraph 3 of this Article the necessary appointments have not been made, either Contracting Party may, in the absence of any other agreement, invite the President of the International Court of Justice to appoint any arbitrator who has or have not yet been appointed. If the President is a national of either Contracting Party or is otherwise prevented from discharging this function, the next most senior member of the International Court of Justice who is not a national of either Contracting Party shall be invited to make the necessary appointments.

5. The arbitral tribunal shall determine its own procedure.

6. The arbitral tribunal shall reach its decision by a majority of votes. The arbitral tribunal shall, upon the request of either Contracting Party, explain the reasons for its decision. Unless otherwise agreed, the arbitral tribunal shall make best efforts to render its decision within six months of the appointment of the Chairman in accordance with paragraphs 3 and 4 of this Article.

7. Each Contracting Party shall bear the cost of its appointed arbitrator and of its representation in the arbitral proceedings. The relevant costs of the Chairman and the arbitral tribunal shall be borne in equal parts by the Contracting Parties.

8. The decision of the arbitral tribunal shall be final and binding on both Contracting Parties. The Contracting Parties shall, if necessary, within 60 days of the decision of an arbitral tribunal, meet and decide on the manner in which to resolve their dispute. That decision shall normally implement the decision of the arbitral tribunal. If the Contracting Parties fail to reach a decision, the Contracting Party bringing the dispute shall be entitled to receive compensation of equivalent value to the arbitral tribunal's award.

Article 16

Denial of Benefits

1. A Contracting Party may, at any time including after the institution of arbitration proceedings in accordance with Part C, deny the benefits of this Agreement to an investor of the other Contracting Party that is an enterprise of that other Contracting Party and to covered investments of that investor:

(a) if investors of a non-Contracting Party own or control the enterprise; and

(b) the denying Contracting Party adopts or maintains measures with respect to the non-Contracting Party:

(i) that prohibit transactions with the enterprise; or

(ii) that would be violated or circumvented if the benefits of this Agreement were accorded to the enterprise or to its covered investments.

2. A Contracting Party may, at any time including after the institution of arbitration proceedings in accordance with Part C, deny the benefits of this Agreement to an investor of the other Contracting Party that is an enterprise of that other Contracting Party and to covered investments of that investor if investors of a non-Contracting Party or of the denying Contracting Party own or control the enterprise and the enterprise has no substantial business activities in the territory of the other Contracting Party under whose law it is constituted or organized.

3. For greater certainty, a Contracting Party may deny the benefits of this Agreement pursuant to paragraphs 1 and 2 at any time, including after the initiation of arbitration proceedings in accordance with Part C.

Article 17

Transparency of Laws, Regulations and Policies

1. Each Contracting Party shall, with a view to promoting the understanding of its laws and policies that pertain to or affect a covered investment:

(a) make such laws and policies public and readily accessible;

(b) if requested, provide copies of specified laws and policies to the other Contracting Party; and

(c) if requested, consult with the other Contracting Party with a view to explaining specified laws and policies.

2. Each Contracting Party shall ensure that its laws, regulations and policies pertaining to the conditions of admission of investments, including procedures for application and registration, criteria used for assessment and approval, timelines for processing an application and rendering a decision, and review or appeal procedures of a decision, are

administered in a manner that enables investors of the other Contracting Party to become acquainted with them.

3. Each Contracting Party is encouraged to:

(a) publish in advance any measure that it proposes to adopt; and

(b) provide interested persons and the other Contracting Party a reasonable opportunity to comment on the proposed measure.

Article 18

Consultations

1. The representatives of the Contracting Parties may hold meetings for the purpose of:

(a) reviewing the implementation of this Agreement;

(b) reviewing the interpretation or application of this Agreement;

(c) exchanging legal information;

(d) addressing disputes arising out of investments;

(e) studying other issues in connection with the facilitation or encouragement of investment, including measures referred to in paragraph 3.

2. Further to consultations under this Article, the Contracting Parties may take any action as they may jointly decide, including making and adopting rules supplementing the applicable arbitral rules under Part C of this Agreement and issuing binding interpretations of this Agreement.

3. The Contracting Parties recognize that it is inappropriate to encourage investment by waiving, relaxing, or otherwise derogating from domestic health, safety or environmental measures.

Part C

Article 19

Purpose

Without prejudice to the rights and obligations of the Contracting Parties under Article 15, this Part establishes a mechanism for the settlement of investment disputes.

Article 20

Claim by an Investor of a Contracting Party

1. An investor of a Contracting Party may submit to arbitration under this Part a claim that the other Contracting Party has breached an obligation:

(a) under Articles 2 to 7(2), 9, 10 to 13, 14(4) or 16, if the breach is with respect to investors or covered investments of investors to which sub paragraph (b) does not apply, or

(b) under Article 10 or 12 if the breach is with respect to investors of a Contracting Party in financial institutions in the other Contracting Party's territory or covered investments of such investors in financial institutions in the other Contracting Party's territory,

and that the investor or a covered investment of the investor has incurred loss or damage by reason of, or arising out of, that breach.

2. (a) Where an investor submits a claim to arbitration under this Article, and the disputing Contracting Party invokes Article 33(3), the investor-State tribunal established pursuant to this Part may not decide whether and to what extent Article 33(3) is a valid defence to the claim of the investor. It shall seek a report in writing from the Contracting Parties on this issue. The investor-State tribunal may not proceed pending receipt of such a report or of a decision of a State-State arbitral tribunal, should such a State-State arbitral tribunal be established.

(b) Pursuant to a request for a report received in accordance with subparagraph (a), the financial services authorities of the Contracting Parties shall engage in consultations. If the financial services authorities of the Contracting Parties reach a joint decision on the issue of whether and to what extent Article 33(3) is a valid defence to the claim of the investor, they shall prepare a written report describing their joint decision. The report shall be transmitted to the investor-State tribunal, and shall be binding on the investor-State tribunal.

(c) If, after 60 days, the financial services authorities of the Contracting Parties are unable to reach a joint decision on the issue of whether and to what extent Article 33(3) is a valid defence to the claim of the investor, the issue shall, within 30 days, be referred by either of the Contracting Parties to a State-State arbitral tribunal established pursuant to Article 15. In such a case, the provisions requiring consultations between the Contracting Parties in Article 15(1) and (2) shall not apply. The decision of the State-State arbitral tribunal shall be transmitted to the investor-State tribunal, and shall be binding on the investor-State tribunal. All of the members of any such State-State arbitral tribunal shall have expertise or experience in financial services law or practice, which may include the regulation of financial institutions.

Article 21

Conditions Precedent to Submission of a Claim to Arbitration

1. Before a disputing investor may submit a claim to arbitration, the disputing parties shall first hold consultations in an attempt to settle a claim amicably. Consultations shall be held within 30 days of the submission of the notice of intent to submit a claim to arbitration, unless the disputing parties otherwise agree. The place of consultation shall be the capital of the disputing Contracting Party, unless the disputing parties otherwise agree.

2. Subject to the Party-specific requirements set out in Annex C.21, a disputing investor may submit a claim to arbitration under Article 20 only if:

(a) the investor consents to arbitration in accordance with the procedures set out in this Agreement and delivers notice of such consent to the disputing Contracting Party together with the submission of a claim to arbitration;

(b) at least six months have elapsed since the events giving rise to the claim;

(c) the investor has delivered to the disputing Contracting Party written notice of its intent to submit a claim to arbitration at least four months prior to submitting the claim;

(d) the investor has delivered, with its notice of intent to submit a claim to arbitration under sub-paragraph (c), evidence establishing that it is an investor of the other Contracting Party;

(e) the investor has waived its right to initiate or continue dispute settlement proceedings under any agreement between a third State and the disputing Contracting Party in relation to the measure alleged to be a breach of an obligation under Part B of this Agreement; and

(f) not more than three years have elapsed from the date on which the investor first acquired, or should have first acquired, knowledge of the alleged breach and knowledge that the investor or a covered investment of the investor has incurred loss or damage thereby.

Article 22

Submission of a Claim to Arbitration

1. A disputing investor who meets the conditions precedent provided for in Article 21 may submit the claim to arbitration under:

(a) the ICSID Convention, provided that both Contracting Parties are parties to that Convention;

(b) the Additional Facility Rules of ICSID, provided that one Contracting Party, but not both, is a party to the ICSID Convention; or

(c) the UNCITRAL Arbitration Rules,

as supplemented or modified by the rules set out in this Agreement or adopted by the Contracting Parties.

2. A claim is submitted to arbitration under this Part when:

(a) the request for arbitration under Article 36(1) of the ICSID Convention is received by the Secretary General;

(b) the notice of arbitration under Article 2 of Schedule C of the ICSID Additional Facility Rules is received by the Secretary General; or

(c) the notice of arbitration given under the UNCITRAL Arbitration Rules is received by the disputing Contracting Party.

3. Delivery of notice and other documents to a Contracting Party shall be made to the place named for that Contracting Party below:

(a)for Canada: Office of the Deputy Attorney General of Canada, Justice Building, 239 Wellington Street, Ottawa, Ontario, K1A 0H8;

(b) for China: Department of Treaty and Law, Ministry of Commerce of the People's Republic of China.

4. The Contracting Parties shall notify each other promptly by diplomatic note of any change in the place for delivery.

Article 23

Consent to Arbitration

Each Contracting Party consents to the submission of a claim to arbitration in accordance with the procedures set out in this Agreement. Failure to meet any of the conditions precedent provided for in Article 21 shall nullify that consent.

Article 24

Arbitrators

1. Except in respect of a Tribunal established under Article 26, and unless the disputing parties agree otherwise, the Tribunal shall comprise three arbitrators, one arbitrator appointed by

each of the disputing parties and the third, who shall be the presiding arbitrator, appointed by agreement of the disputing parties.

2. Arbitrators shall:

(a) have expertise or experience in public international law, international trade or international investment rules, or the resolution of disputes arising under international trade or international investment agreements;

(b) be independent of, and not be affiliated with, or take instructions from, either Contracting Party or disputing party; and

(c) comply with any additional rules where such rules are agreed to by the Contracting Parties.

3. Where the claimant claims that a dispute involves measures adopted or maintained by the disputing Contracting Party relating to financial institutions of the other Contracting Party, or investors of the other Contracting Party and covered investments of such investors in financial institutions in the disputing Contracting Party's territory, then:

(a) where the disputing parties are in agreement, the arbitrators shall, in addition to the criteria set out in paragraph 2, have expertise or experience in financial services law or practice, which may include the regulation of financial institutions; or

(b) where the disputing parties are not in agreement,

(i) each disputing party may select arbitrators who meet the qualifications set out in subparagraph (a), and

(ii) if the disputing Contracting Party invokes Article 33(4), the presiding arbitrator shall meet the qualifications set out in subparagraph (a).

4. If the disputing parties do not agree on the remuneration of the arbitrators before the constitution of the Tribunal, the prevailing ICSID rate for arbitrators shall apply.

5. If a Tribunal, other than a Tribunal established under Article 26, has not been constituted within 90 days from the date that a claim is submitted to arbitration, the Secretary General of ICSID, on the request of either disputing party, shall appoint, in his or her discretion, the arbitrator or arbitrators not yet appointed, except that the presiding arbitrator shall not be a national of either Contracting Party.

Article 25

Agreement to Appointment of Arbitrators

For the purposes of Article 39 of the ICSID Convention and Article 7 of Schedule C to the Additional Facility Rules of ICSID, and without prejudice to an objection to an arbitrator based on a ground other than citizenship or permanent residence:

(a) the disputing Contracting Party agrees to the appointment of each individual member of a Tribunal established under the ICSID Convention or the Additional Facility Rules of ICSID;

(b) a disputing investor may submit a claim to arbitration, or continue a claim, under the ICSID Convention or the Additional Facility Rules of ICSID, only on condition that the disputing investor agrees in writing to the appointment of each individual member of the Tribunal.

Article 26

Consolidation

1. Where two or more claims have been submitted separately to arbitration under Article 20 and the claims have a question of law or fact in common and arise out of the same events or circumstances, any disputing party may seek a consolidation order in accordance with either the agreement of all the disputing parties sought to be covered by the order, or the terms of paragraphs 2 through 9.

2. A disputing party that seeks a consolidation order under this Article shall deliver, in writing, a request to the Secretary-General of ICSID and to all the disputing parties sought to be covered by the order and shall specify in the request: the names

and addresses of all the disputing parties sought to be covered by the order; the nature of the order sought; and the grounds on which the order is sought.

3. Unless the Secretary-General of ICSID finds within 30 days after receiving a request under paragraph 2 that the request is manifestly unfounded, a tribunal shall be established under this Article.

4. Unless all the disputing parties sought to be covered by the order otherwise agree, a tribunal established under this Article shall comprise three arbitrators: one arbitrator appointed by agreement of the claimants; one arbitrator appointed by the respondent; and the presiding arbitrator appointed by the Secretary-General of ICSID, provided, however, that the presiding arbitrator shall not be a national of either Contracting Party.

5. If, within 60 days after the Secretary-General of ICSID receives a request made under paragraph 2, the disputing Contracting Party fails or the claimants fail to appoint an arbitrator in accordance with paragraph 4, the Secretary-General of ICSID, at the request of any disputing party sought to be covered by the order, shall appoint the arbitrator or arbitrators not yet appointed.

6. Where a tribunal established under this Article is satisfied that two or more claims that have been submitted to arbitration under Article 20 have a question of law or fact in common, and arise out of the same events or circumstances, the tribunal may, in the interest of fair and efficient resolution of the claims, and after hearing the disputing parties, by order: assume jurisdiction over, and hear and determine together, all or part of the claims; or assume jurisdiction over, and hear and determine one or more of the claims, the determination of which it believes would assist in the resolution of the others.

7. A tribunal established under this Article shall conduct its proceedings in accordance with the UNCITRAL Arbitration Rules, except as modified by this Section.

8. A tribunal established under Articles 22 through 25 shall not have jurisdiction to decide a claim, or a part of a claim, over which a tribunal established under this Article has assumed jurisdiction.

9. On application of a disputing party, a tribunal established under this Article may, pending its decision under paragraph 6, order that the proceedings of a tribunal established under Article 22 through 25 be stayed, unless the latter tribunal has already adjourned its proceedings.

Article 27

The Non-Disputing Contracting Party: Documents and Participation

1. A disputing Contracting Party shall deliver to the other Contracting Party a copy of the notice of intent to submit a claim to arbitration, and the relevant document submitted pursuant to Article 22(2) no later than 30 days after the date that such documents have been delivered to the disputing Contracting Party. The non-disputing Contracting Party shall be entitled, at its cost, to receive from the disputing Contracting Party a copy of the evidence that has been tendered to the Tribunal, copies of all pleadings filed in the arbitration, and the written argument of the disputing parties. The Contracting Party receiving such information shall treat the information as if it were a disputing Contracting Party.

2. The non-disputing Contracting Party shall have the right to attend any hearings held under this Part of this Agreement. Upon written notice to the disputing parties, the non-disputing Contracting Party may make submissions to a Tribunal on a question of interpretation of this Agreement.

Article 28

Public Access to Hearings and Documents

1. Any Tribunal award under this Part shall be publicly available, subject to the redaction of confidential information. Where a disputing Contracting Party determines that it is in

the public interest to do so and notifies the Tribunal of that determination, all other documents submitted to, or issued by, the Tribunal shall also be publicly available, subject to the redaction of confidential information.

2. Where, after consulting with a disputing investor, a disputing Contracting Party determines that it is in the public interest to do so and notifies the Tribunal of that determination, hearings held under this Part shall be open to the public. To the extent necessary to ensure the protection of confidential information, including business confidential information, the Tribunal may hold portions of hearings in camera.

3. A disputing party may disclose to other persons in connection with the arbitral proceedings such unredacted documents as it considers necessary for the preparation of its case, but it shall ensure that those persons protect the confidential information in such documents.

4. The Contracting Parties may share with officials of their respective federal and sub-national governments all relevant unredacted documents in the course of dispute settlement under this Agreement, but they shall ensure that those persons protect any confidential information in such documents.

5. To the extent that a Tribunal's confidentiality order designates information as confidential and a Contracting Party's law on access to information requires public access to that information, the Contracting Party's law on access to information shall prevail. However, a Contracting Party should endeavour to apply its law on access to information so as to protect information designated confidential by the Tribunal.

Article 29

Submissions by a Non-Disputing Party

A Tribunal, after consultation with the disputing parties, may accept written submissions from a person or entity that is not a disputing party if that non-disputing party has a significant interest in the arbitration. The Tribunal shall ensure that any non disputing party submission does not disrupt the proceedings and that neither disputing party is unduly burdened or unfairly prejudiced by it.

An application to the Tribunal for leave to file a non-disputing party submission, and the filing of a submission, if allowed by the Tribunal, shall be made in accordance with Annex C.29.

Article 30

Governing Law

1. A Tribunal established under this Part shall decide the issues in dispute in accordance with this Agreement, and applicable rules of international law, and where relevant and as appropriate, take into consideration the law of the host Contracting Party. An interpretation by the Contracting Parties of a provision of this Agreement shall be binding on a Tribunal established under this Part, and any award under this Part shall be consistent with such interpretation.

2. Where a disputing Contracting Party asserts as a defence that the measure alleged to be a breach is within the scope of the reservations and exceptions set out in Article 8(1), (2) and (3), on request of the disputing Contracting Party, the Tribunal shall request the interpretation of the Contracting Parties on the issue. The Contracting Parties, within 60 days of delivery of the request, shall submit in writing their joint interpretation to the Tribunal. The interpretation shall be binding on the Tribunal. If the Contracting Parties fail to submit an interpretation within 60 days, the Tribunal shall decide the issue.

Article 31

Interim Measures of Protection and Final Award

1. A Tribunal may recommend an interim measure of protection to preserve the rights of a disputing party, or to ensure that the Tribunal's jurisdiction is made fully effective, including a recommendation to preserve evidence in the possession or control of a disputing party or to protect the Tribunal's jurisdiction. A Tribunal shall not recommend attachment or

enjoin the application of the measure alleged to constitute a breach referred to in Article 20.

2. Where a Tribunal makes a final award against the disputing Contracting Party, the Tribunal may award, separately or in combination, and subject to the requirements in paragraph 3, only:

(a) monetary damages and any applicable interest;

(b) restitution of property, in which case the award shall provide that the disputing Contracting Party may pay monetary damages and any applicable interest in lieu of restitution.

The Tribunal may also award costs in accordance with the applicable arbitration rules.

3. Where a claim is made for damages to a covered investment that is a juridical person that the investor owns or controls:

(a) an award of monetary damages and any applicable interest shall provide that the sum be paid to that covered investment;

(b) an award of restitution of property shall provide that restitution be made to that covered investment; and

(c) the award shall provide that it is made without prejudice to any right that any person may have in the relief under applicable domestic law.

4. A Tribunal shall not order a disputing Contracting Party to pay punitive damages.

Article 32

Finality and Enforcement of an Award

1. An award made by a Tribunal shall have no binding force except between the disputing parties and in respect of that particular case.

2. Subject to paragraph 3 and the applicable review procedure for an interim award, a disputing party shall abide by and comply with an award without delay.

3. A disputing party may not seek enforcement of a final award until:

(a) in the case of a final award made under the ICSID Convention:

(i) 120 days have elapsed from the date the award was rendered, provided that a disputing party has not requested the award be revised or annulled, or

(ii) revision or annulment proceedings have been completed; and

(b) in the case of a final award under the ICSID Additional Facility Rules or the UNCITRAL Arbitration Rules:

(i) 90 days have elapsed from the date the award was rendered and no disputing party has commenced a proceeding to revise, set aside or annul the award, or

(ii) a court has dismissed or allowed an application to revise, set aside or annul the award and there is no further appeal.

4. Each Contracting Party shall provide for the enforcement of an award in its territory.

Part D

Article 33

General Exceptions

1. Nothing in this Agreement shall apply to measures in respect of cultural industries. "Cultural industries" means natural persons or enterprises engaged in any of the following activities:

(a) the publication, distribution, or sale of books, magazines, periodicals or newspapers in print or machine readable form but does not include the sole activity of printing or typesetting any of the foregoing;

(b) the production, distribution, sale or exhibition of film or video recordings;

(c) the production, distribution, sale or exhibition of audio or video music recordings;

(d) the publication, distribution, sale or exhibition of music in print or machine readable form; or

(e) radiocommunications in which the transmissions are intended for direct reception by the general public, and all radio, television or cable broadcasting undertakings and all satellite programming and broadcast network services.

2. Provided that such measures are not applied in an arbitrary or unjustifiable manner, or do not constitute a disguised restriction on international trade or investment, nothing in this Agreement shall be construed to prevent a Contracting Party from adopting or maintaining measures, including environmental measures:

(a) necessary to ensure compliance with laws and regulations that are not inconsistent with the provisions of this Agreement;

(b) necessary to protect human, animal or plant life or health; or

(c) relating to the conservation of living or non-living exhaustible natural resources if such measures are made effective in conjunction with restrictions on domestic production or consumption.

3. Nothing in this Agreement shall be construed to prevent a Contracting Party from adopting or maintaining reasonable measures for prudential reasons, such as:

(a) the protection of depositors, financial market participants and investors9, policy-holders, policy-claimants, or persons to whom a fiduciary duty is owed by a financial institution;

(b) the maintenance of the safety, soundness, integrity or financial responsibility of financial institutions; and

(c) ensuring the integrity and stability of a Contracting Party's financial system.

4. Nothing in this Agreement shall apply to non-discriminatory measures of general application taken by any public entity10 in pursuit of monetary and related credit policies or exchange rate policies. This paragraph shall not affect a Contracting Party's obligations under Article 12.

5. Nothing in this Agreement shall be construed:

(a) to require a Contracting Party to furnish or allow access to any information if the Contracting Party determines that the disclosure of that information is contrary to its essential security interests;

(b) to prevent a Contracting Party from taking any actions that it considers necessary for the protection of its essential security interests:

(i) relating to the traffic in arms, ammunition and implements of war and to such traffic and transactions in other goods, materials, services and technology undertaken directly or indirectly for the purpose of supplying a military or other security establishment,

(ii) in time of war or other emergency in international relations, or

(iii) relating to the implementation of national policies or international agreements respecting the non-proliferation of nuclear weapons or other nuclear explosive devices; or

(c) to prevent a Contracting Party from taking action in pursuance of its obligations under the United Nations Charter for the maintenance of international peace and security.

6. (a) Nothing in this Agreement shall be construed to require a Contracting Party to furnish or allow access to information the disclosure of which would impede law enforcement or would be contrary to the Contracting Party's law protecting Cabinet confidences, personal privacy or the confidentiality of the financial affairs and accounts of individual customers of financial institutions.

(b) Nothing in this Agreement shall be construed to require, during the course of any dispute settlement procedure under this Agreement, a Contracting Party to furnish or allow access to information protected under its competition laws, or a competition authority of a Contracting Party to furnish or allow access to any other information that is privileged or otherwise protected from disclosure.

(c) In subparagraph (b),

"competition authority" means the following until otherwise notified by a Contracting Party:

(i) for Canada, the Commissioner of Competition; and

(ii) for China, the authority for enforcement of anti-monopoly law under the State Council.

The Contracting Parties shall notify each other promptly by diplomatic note of the successors to the competition authorities identified in sub paragraphs (i) and (ii).

"information protected under its competition laws" means:

(i) for Canada, information within the scope of section 29 of the Competition Act, R.S. 1985, c.34, or any successor provision; and

(ii) for China, information protected from disclosure under the relevant provisions of the Anti-Monopoly Law, the Pricing Law and the Law Against Unfair Competition, or any successor provisions.

7. Any measure adopted by a Contracting Party in conformity with a decision adopted by the World Trade Organization pursuant to Article IX:3 of the WTO Agreement shall be deemed to be also in conformity with this Agreement. An investor purporting to act pursuant to Article 20 of this Agreement may not claim that such a conforming measure is in breach of this Agreement.

Article 34

Exclusions

Article 15 and Part C of this Agreement do not apply to the decisions set out in Annex D.34.

Article 35

Entry into Force and Termination

1. The Contracting Parties shall notify each other through diplomatic channels that they have completed the internal legal procedures for the entry into force of this Agreement. This Agreement shall enter into force on the first day of the following month after the second notification is received, and shall remain in force for a period of at least fifteen years.

2. After the expiration of the initial fifteen-year period, this Agreement shall continue to be in force. Either Contracting Party may at any time thereafter terminate this Agreement. The termination will be effective one year after notice of termination has been received by the other Contracting Party.

3. With respect to investments made prior to the date of termination of this Agreement, Articles 1 to 34, as well as paragraph 4 of this Article, shall continue to be effective for an additional fifteen-year period from the date of termination.

4. The Annexes and footnotes to this Agreement constitute integral parts of this Agreement.

IN WITNESS WHEREOF, the duly authorized representatives of their respective Governments have signed this Agreement.

ANNEXES

Annex B.8

Exceptions

1. Canada reserves the right to adopt or maintain any measure that does not conform to the obligations in Articles 5, 6 or 7, provided that in the Schedule of Canada, including its headnote,

in Annex II to the Free Trade Agreement between Canada and the Republic of Peru, as done at Lima on 29 May 2008, Canada reserved the right to adopt or maintain that measure in respect of investors or investments of investors of Peru. For greater certainty, this right is reserved even if the Canada-Peru Free Trade Agreement is no longer in force.

2. China reserves the right to adopt or maintain any measure that does not conform to the obligations in Articles 5, 6 or 7, provided that in Chapter 10 of the Free Trade Agreement between China and the Republic of Peru, as done at Beijing on 28 April 2008, China reserved the right to adopt or maintain that measure in respect of investors or investments of investors of Peru. For greater certainty, this right is reserved even if the China-Peru Free Trade Agreement is no longer in force.

Annex B.10

Expropriation

The Contracting Parties confirm their shared understanding that:

1. Indirect expropriation results from a measure or series of measures of a Contracting Party that has an effect equivalent to direct expropriation without formal transfer of title or outright seizure.

2. The determination of whether a measure or series of measures of a Contracting Party constitutes an indirect expropriation requires a case-by-case, fact-based inquiry that considers, among other factors:

(a) the economic impact of the measure or series of measures, although the sole fact that a measure or series of measures of a Contracting Party has an adverse effect on the economic value of an investment does not establish that an indirect expropriation has occurred;

(b) the extent to which the measure or series of measures interferes with distinct, reasonable, investment-backed expectations; and

(c) the character of the measure or series of measures.

3. Except in rare circumstances, such as if a measure or series of measures is so severe in light of its purpose that it cannot be reasonably viewed as having been adopted and applied in good faith, a non-discriminatory measure or series of measures of a Contracting Party that is designed and applied to protect the legitimate public objectives for the well-being of citizens, such as health, safety and the environment, does not constitute indirect expropriation.

Annex B.12

Transfers and Exchange Formalities

With regards to China:

1. The obligations in Article 12(1) shall apply provided that the transfer complies with the relevant formalities stipulated by the present laws and regulations of China relating to exchange control. These formalities:

(a) shall not be used as a means of avoiding China's commitments or obligations under this Agreement; and

(b) shall not be made more restrictive than the formalities required at the time when original investment was made.

2. With respect to these formalities, China shall accord to investors of Canada or covered investments of Canadian investors treatment no less favourable than the treatment that China accords to third country investors or investments of such investors. To the extent that these formalities are no longer required according to the relevant laws of China, Article 12(1) shall apply without restrictions.

3. A transfer shall be deemed to have been made 'without delay' within the meaning of Article 12(1) if effected within such period as is normally required for the completion of transfer formalities. The said period shall commence on the day on which the relevant request has been submitted to the relevant foreign exchange administration with full and

authentic documentation and information and may not exceed two months.

Annex C.21

Conditions Precedent to Submission of a Claim to Arbitration: Party-Specific Requirements

Where the claim concerns a measure of China:

1. Upon receipt of the Notice of Intent or at any time prior, China shall require that an investor make use of the domestic administrative reconsideration procedure. If the investor considers that the dispute still exists four months11 after the investor has applied for the administrative reconsideration, or where no such remedies are available, the investor may submit its claim to arbitration.

2. An investor who has initiated proceedings before any court of China with respect to the measure of China alleged to be a breach of an obligation under Part B may only submit a claim to arbitration under Article 20 if the investor has withdrawn the case from the national court before judgment has been made on the dispute. This requirement does not apply to the domestic administrative reconsideration procedure referred to in paragraph 1.

Where the claim concerns a measure of Canada:

3. The investor and, where the claim is for loss or damage to an interest in an enterprise of Canada that is a juridical person that the investor owns or controls directly or indirectly, the enterprise shall waive their right to initiate or continue before any administrative tribunal or court under the law of any Contracting Party, or other dispute settlement procedures, any proceedings with respect to the measure of Canada that is alleged to be a breach referred to in Article 20, except for proceedings for injunctive, declaratory or other extraordinary relief, not involving the payment of damages, before an administrative tribunal or court under the law of Canada.

4. The waiver required under paragraph 3 shall be delivered to Canada and shall be included in the submission of a claim to arbitration. A waiver from the enterprise shall not be required if Canada has deprived a disputing investor of control of an enterprise.

Annex C.29

Submissions by Non-Disputing Parties

1. The application for leave to file a non-disputing party submission shall:

(a) be made in writing, dated and signed by the person filing the application, and include the address and other contact details of the applicant;

(b) be no longer than 5 typed pages;

(c) describe the applicant, including, where relevant, its membership and legal status (e.g., company, trade association or other non-governmental organization), its general objectives, the nature of its activities, and any parent organization (including any organization that directly or indirectly controls the applicant);

(d) disclose whether the applicant has any affiliation, direct or indirect, with any disputing party;

(e) identify any government, person or organization that has provided any financial or other assistance in preparing the submission;

(f) specify the nature of the interest that the applicant has in the arbitration, including an explanation of how the submission would assist the Tribunal in the determination of a factual or legal issue related to the proceedings by bringing a perspective, particular knowledge or insight that is different from that of the disputing parties;

(g) identify the specific issues of fact or law in the arbitration that the applicant has addressed in its written submission; and

(h) be made in a language of the arbitration.

2. The submission filed by a non-disputing party shall:

(a) be dated and signed by the person filing the submission;

(b) be concise, and in no case longer than 20 typed pages, including any appendices;

(c) set out a precise statement supporting the applicant's position on the issues; and

(d) only address matters within the scope of the dispute.

Annex D.34

Exclusions

1. A decision by Canada following a review under the Investment Canada Act, an Act respecting investment in Canada, with respect to whether or not to:

(a) initially approve an investment12 that is subject to review; or

(b) permit an investment that is subject to national security review;

shall not be subject to the dispute settlement provisions under Article 15 and Part C of this Agreement.

2. A decision by China following a review under the Laws, Regulations and Rules relating to the regulation of foreign investment, with respect to whether or not to:

(a) initially approve an investment that is subject to review; or

(b) permit an investment that is subject to national security review13;

shall not be subject to the dispute settlement provisions under Article 15 and Part C of this Agreement.

ANNEX 2: Relevant Legislation, Rules and Guidelines

(i) Extracts of ICSID Convention

CONVENTION ON THE SETTLEMENT OF INVESTMENT DISPUTES BETWEEN STATES AND NATIONALS OF OTHER STATES

Preamble

The Contracting States

Considering the need for international cooperation for economic development, and the role of private international investment therein;

Bearing in mind the possibility that from time to time disputes may arise in connection with such investment between Contracting States and nationals of other Contracting States;

Recognizing that while such disputes would usually be subject to national legal processes, international methods of settlement may be appropriate in certain cases;

Attaching particular importance to the availability of facilities for international conciliation or arbitration to which Contracting States and nationals of other Contracting States may submit such disputes if they so desire;

Desiring to establish such facilities under the auspices of the International Bank for Reconstruction and Development;

Recognizing that mutual consent by the parties to submit such disputes to conciliation or to arbitration through such facilities constitutes a binding agreement which requires in particular that due consideration be given to any recommendation of conciliators, and that any arbitral award be complied with; and

Declaring that no Contracting State shall by the mere fact of its ratification, acceptance or approval of this Convention and without its consent be deemed to be under any obligation to submit any particular dispute to conciliation or arbitration,

Have agreed as follows:

Article 1

(1) There is hereby established the International Centre for Settlement of Investment Disputes (hereinafter called the Centre).

(2) The purpose of the Centre shall be to provide facilities for conciliation and arbitration of investment disputes between Contracting States and nationals of other Contracting States in accordance with the provisions of this Convention.

Article 2

The seat of the Centre shall be at the principal office of the International Bank for Reconstruction and Development (hereinafter called the Bank). The seat may be moved to another place by decision of the Administrative Council adopted by a majority of two-thirds of its members.

Article 3

The Centre shall have an Administrative Council and a Secretariat and shall maintain a Panel of Conciliators and a Panel of Arbitrators.

Section 4

The Panels

Article 12

The Panel of Conciliators and the Panel of Arbitrators shall each consist of qualified persons, designated as hereinafter provided, who are willing to serve thereon.

Article 13

(1) Each Contracting State may designate to each Panel four persons who may but need not be its nationals.

(2) The Chairman may designate ten persons to each Panel. The persons so designated to a Panel shall each have a different nationality.

Article 14

(1) Persons designated to serve on the Panels shall be persons of high moral character and recognized competence in the fields of law, commerce, industry or finance, who may be relied upon to exercise independent judgment. Competence in the field of law shall be of particular importance in the case of persons on the Panel of Arbitrators.

(2) The Chairman, in designating persons to serve on the Panels, shall in addition pay due regard to the importance of assuring representation on the Panels of the principal legal systems of the world and of the main forms of economic activity.

Article 15

(1) Panel members shall serve for renewable periods of six years.

(2) In case of death or resignation of a member of a Panel, the authority which designated the member shall have the right to designate another person to serve for the remainder of that member's term.

(3) Panel members shall continue in office until their successors have been designated.

Article 16

(1) A person may serve on both Panels.

(2) If a person shall have been designated to serve on the same Panel by more than one Contracting State, or by one or more Contracting States and the Chairman, he shall be deemed to have been designated by the authority which first designated him or, if one such authority is the State of which he is a national, by that State.

(3) All designations shall be notified to the Secretary-General and shall take effect from the date on which the notification is received.

Section 6

Status, Immunities and Privileges

Article 21

The Chairman, the members of the Administrative Council, persons acting as conciliators or arbitrators or members of a Committee appointed pursuant to paragraph (3) of Article 52, and the officers and employees of the Secretariat

(a) shall enjoy immunity from legal process with respect to acts performed by them in the exercise of their functions, except when the Centre waives this immunity;

(b) not being local nationals, shall enjoy the same immunities from immigration restrictions, alien registration requirements and national service obligations, the same facilities as regards exchange restrictions and the same treatment in respect of travelling facilities as are accorded by Contracting States to the representatives, officials and employees of comparable rank of other Contracting States.

Article 22

The provisions of Article 21 shall apply to persons appearing in proceedings under this Convention as parties, agents, counsel, advocates, witnesses or experts; provided, however, that sub-paragraph (b) thereof shall apply only in connection with their travel to and from, and their stay at, the place where the proceedings are held.

Chapter II

Jurisdiction of the Centre

Article 25

(1) The jurisdiction of the Centre shall extend to any legal dispute arising directly out of an investment, between a Contracting State (or any constituent subdivision or agency of a Contracting State designated to the Centre by that State) and

a national of another Contracting State, which the parties to the dispute consent in writing to submit to the Centre. When the parties have given their consent, no party may withdraw its consent unilaterally.

(2) "National of another Contracting State" means:

(a) any natural person who had the nationality of a Contracting State other than the State party to the dispute on the date on which the parties consented to submit such dispute to conciliation or arbitration as well as on the date on which the request was registered pursuant to paragraph (3) of Article 28 or paragraph (3) of Article 36, but does not include any person who on either date also had the nationality of the Contracting State party to the dispute; and

(b) any juridical person which had the nationality of a Contracting

State other than the State party to the dispute on the date on which the parties consented to submit such dispute to conciliation or arbitration and any juridical person which had the nationality of the Contracting State party to the dispute on that date and which, because of foreign control, the parties have agreed should be treated as a national of another Contracting State for the purposes of this Convention.

(3) Consent by a constituent subdivision or agency of a Contracting State shall require the approval of that State unless that State notifies the Centre that no such approval is required.

(4) Any Contracting State may, at the time of ratification, acceptance or approval of this Convention or at any time thereafter, notify the Centre of the class or classes of disputes which it would or would not consider submitting to the jurisdiction of the Centre. The Secretary- General shall forthwith transmit such notification to all Contracting States. Such notification shall not constitute the consent required by paragraph (1).

Article 26

Consent of the parties to arbitration under this Convention shall, unless otherwise stated, be deemed consent to such arbitration to the exclusion of any other remedy. A Contracting State may require the exhaustion of local administrative or judicial remedies as a condition of its consent to arbitration under this Convention.

Article 27

(1) No Contracting State shall give diplomatic protection, or bring an international claim, in respect of a dispute which one of its nationals and another Contracting State shall have consented to submit or shall have submitted to arbitration under this Convention, unless such other Contracting State shall have failed to abide by and comply with the award rendered in such dispute.

(2) Diplomatic protection, for the purposes of paragraph (1), shall not include informal diplomatic exchanges for the sole purpose of facilitating a settlement of the dispute.

Chapter IV

Arbitration

Section 1

Request for Arbitration

Article 36

(1) Any Contracting State or any national of a Contracting State wishing to institute arbitration proceedings shall address a request to that effect in writing to the Secretary-General who shall send a copy of the request to the other party.

(2) The request shall contain information concerning the issues in dispute, the identity of the parties and their consent to arbitration in accordance with the rules of procedure for the institution of conciliation and arbitration proceedings.

(3) The Secretary-General shall register the request unless he finds, on the basis of the information contained in the request, that the dispute is manifestly outside the jurisdiction of the Centre. He shall forthwith notify the parties of registration or refusal to register.

Section 2

Constitution of the Tribunal

Article 37

(1) The Arbitral Tribunal (hereinafter called the Tribunal) shall be constituted as soon as possible after registration of a request pursuant to Article 36.

(2) (a) The Tribunal shall consist of a sole arbitrator or any uneven number of arbitrators appointed as the parties shall agree.

(b) Where the parties do not agree upon the number of arbitrators and the method of their appointment, the Tribunal shall consist of three arbitrators, one arbitrator appointed by each party and the third, who shall be the president of the Tribunal, appointed by agreement of the parties.

Article 38

If the Tribunal shall not have been constituted within 90 days after notice of registration of the request has been dispatched by the Secretary-General in accordance with paragraph (3) of Article 36, or such other period as the parties may agree, the Chairman shall, at the request of either party and after consulting both parties as far as possible, appoint the arbitrator or arbitrators not yet appointed. Arbitrators appointed by the Chairman pursuant to this Article shall not be nationals of the Contracting State party to the dispute or of the Contracting State whose national is a party to the dispute.

Article 39

The majority of the arbitrators shall be nationals of States other than the Contracting State party to the dispute and the

Contracting State whose national is a party to the dispute; provided, however, that the foregoing provisions of this Article shall not apply if the sole arbitrator or each individual member of the Tribunal has been appointed by agreement of the parties.

Article 40

(1) Arbitrators may be appointed from outside the Panel of Arbitrators, except in the case of appointments by the Chairman pursuant to Article 38.

(2) Arbitrators appointed from outside the Panel of Arbitrators shall possess the qualities stated in paragraph (1) of Article 14.

Section 3

Powers and Functions of the Tribunal

Article 41

(1) The Tribunal shall be the judge of its own competence.

(2) Any objection by a party to the dispute that that dispute is not within the jurisdiction of the Centre, or for other reasons is not within the competence of the Tribunal, shall be considered by the Tribunal which shall determine whether to deal with it as a preliminary question or to join it to the merits of the dispute.

Article 42

(1) The Tribunal shall decide a dispute in accordance with such rules of law as may be agreed by the parties. In the absence of such agreement, the Tribunal shall apply the law of the Contracting State party to the dispute (including its rules on the conflict of laws) and such rules of international law as may be applicable.

(2) The Tribunal may not bring in a finding of non liquet on the ground of silence or obscurity of the law.

(3) The provisions of paragraphs (1) and (2) shall not prejudice the power of the Tribunal to decide a dispute ex aequo et bono if the parties so agree.

Article 43

Except as the parties otherwise agree, the Tribunal may, if it deems it necessary at any stage of the proceedings,

(a) call upon the parties to produce documents or other evidence, and

(b) visit the scene connected with the dispute, and conduct such inquiries there as it may deem appropriate.

Article 44

Any arbitration proceeding shall be conducted in accordance with the provisions of this Section and, except as the parties otherwise agree, in accordance with the Arbitration Rules in effect on the date on which the parties consented to arbitration. If any question of procedure arises which is not covered by this Section or the Arbitration Rules or any rules agreed by the parties, the Tribunal shall decide the question.

Article 45

(1) Failure of a party to appear or to present his case shall not be deemed an admission of the other party's assertions.

(2) If a party fails to appear or to present his case at any stage of the proceedings the other party may request the Tribunal to deal with the questions submitted to it and to render an award. Before rendering an award, the Tribunal shall notify, and grant a period of grace to, the party failing to appear or to present its case, unless it is satisfied that that party does not intend to do so.

Article 46

Except as the parties otherwise agree, the Tribunal shall, if requested by a party, determine any incidental or additional claims or counterclaims arising directly out of the subject-matter of the dispute provided that they are within the scope of the consent of the parties and are otherwise within the jurisdiction of the Centre.

Article 47

Except as the parties otherwise agree, the Tribunal may, if it considers that the circumstances so require, recommend any provisional measures which should be taken to preserve the respective rights of either party.

Section 4

The Award

Article 48

(1) The Tribunal shall decide questions by a majority of the votes of all its members.

(2) The award of the Tribunal shall be in writing and shall be signed by the members of the Tribunal who voted for it.

(3) The award shall deal with every question submitted to the Tribunal, and shall state the reasons upon which it is based.

(4) Any member of the Tribunal may attach his individual opinion to the award, whether he dissents from the majority or not, or a statement of his dissent.

(5) The Centre shall not publish the award without the consent of the parties.

Article 49

(1) The Secretary-General shall promptly dispatch certified copies of the award to the parties. The award shall be deemed to have been rendered on the date on which the certified copies were dispatched.

(2) The Tribunal upon the request of a party made within 45 days after the date on which the award was rendered may after notice to the other party decide any question which it had omitted to decide in the award, and shall rectify any clerical, arithmetical or similar error in the award. Its decision shall become part of the award and shall be notified to the parties in the same manner as the award. The periods of time provided for under paragraph (2) of Article 51 and paragraph (2) of

Article 52 shall run from the date on which the decision was rendered.

Section 5

Interpretation, Revision and Annulment of the Award

Article 50

(1) If any dispute shall arise between the parties as to the meaning or scope of an award, either party may request interpretation of the award by an application in writing addressed to the Secretary-General.

(2) The request shall, if possible, be submitted to the Tribunal which rendered the award. If this shall not be possible, a new Tribunal shall be constituted in accordance with Section 2 of this Chapter. The Tribunal may, if it considers that the circumstances so require, stay enforcement of the award pending its decision.

Article 51

(1) Either party may request revision of the award by an application in writing addressed to the Secretary-General on the ground of discovery of some fact of such a nature as decisively to affect the award, provided that when the award was rendered that fact was unknown to the Tribunal and to the applicant and that the applicant's ignorance of that fact was not due to negligence.

(2) The application shall be made within 90 days after the discovery of such fact and in any event within three years after the date on which the award was rendered.

(3) The request shall, if possible, be submitted to the Tribunal which rendered the award. If this shall not be possible, a new Tribunal shall be constituted in accordance with Section 2 of this Chapter.

(4) The Tribunal may, if it considers that the circumstances so require, stay enforcement of the award pending its decision. If the applicant requests a stay of enforcement of the award in his

application, enforcement shall be stayed provisionally until the Tribunal rules on such request.

Article 52

(1) Either party may request annulment of the award by an application in writing addressed to the Secretary-General on one or more of the following grounds:

(a) that the Tribunal was not properly constituted;

(b) that the Tribunal has manifestly exceeded its powers;

(c) that there was corruption on the part of a member of the Tribunal;

(d) that there has been a serious departure from a fundamental rule of procedure; or

(e) that the award has failed to state the reasons on which it is based.

(2) The application shall be made within 120 days after the date on which the award was rendered except that when annulment is requested on the ground of corruption such application shall be made within 120 days after discovery of the corruption and in any event within three years after the date on which the award was rendered.

(3) On receipt of the request the Chairman shall forthwith appoint from the Panel of Arbitrators an ad hoc Committee of three persons.

None of the members of the Committee shall have been a member of the Tribunal which rendered the award, shall be of the same nationality as any such member, shall be a national of the State party to the dispute or of the State whose national is a party to the dispute, shall have been designated to the Panel of Arbitrators by either of those States, or shall have acted as a conciliator in the same dispute. The Committee shall have the authority to annul the award or any part thereof on any of the grounds set forth in paragraph (1).

(4) The provisions of Articles 41-45, 48, 49, 53 and 54, and of Chapters VI and VII shall apply mutatis mutandis to proceedings before the Committee.

(5) The Committee may, if it considers that the circumstances so require, stay enforcement of the award pending its decision. If the applicant requests a stay of enforcement of the award in his application, enforcement shall be stayed provisionally until the Committee rules on such request.

(6) If the award is annulled the dispute shall, at the request of either party, be submitted to a new Tribunal constituted in accordance with Section 2 of this Chapter.

Section 6

Recognition and Enforcement of the Award

Article 53

(1) The award shall be binding on the parties and shall not be subject to any appeal or to any other remedy except those provided for in this Convention. Each party shall abide by and comply with the terms of the award except to the extent that enforcement shall have been stayed pursuant to the relevant provisions of this Convention.

(2) For the purposes of this Section, "award" shall include any decision interpreting, revising or annulling such award pursuant to Articles 50, 51 or 52.

Article 54

(1) Each Contracting State shall recognize an award rendered pursuant to this Convention as binding and enforce the pecuniary obligations imposed by that award within its territories as if it were a final judgment of a court in that State. A Contracting State with a federal constitution may enforce such an award in or through its federal courts and may provide that such courts shall treat the award as if it were a final judgment of the courts of a constituent state.

(2) A party seeking recognition or enforcement in the territories of a Contracting State shall furnish to a competent court or other authority which such State shall have designated for this purpose a copy of the award certified by the Secretary-General. Each Contracting State shall notify the Secretary-General of the designation of the competent court or other authority for this purpose and of any subsequent change in such designation.

(3) Execution of the award shall be governed by the laws concerning the execution of judgments in force in the State in whose territories such execution is sought.

Article 55

Nothing in Article 54 shall be construed as derogating from the law in force in any Contracting State relating to immunity of that State or of any foreign State from execution.

Chapter V

Replacement and Disqualification of Conciliators and Arbitrators

Article 56

(1) After a Commission or a Tribunal has been constituted and proceedings have begun, its composition shall remain unchanged; provided, however, that if a conciliator or an arbitrator should die, become incapacitated, or resign, the resulting vacancy shall be filled in accordance with the provisions of Section 2 of Chapter III or Section 2 of Chapter IV.

(2) A member of a Commission or Tribunal shall continue to serve in that capacity notwithstanding that he shall have ceased to be a member of the Panel.

(3) If a conciliator or arbitrator appointed by a party shall have resigned without the consent of the Commission or Tribunal of which he was a member, the Chairman shall appoint a person from the appropriate Panel to fill the resulting vacancy.

Article 57

A party may propose to a Commission or Tribunal the disqualification of any of its members on account of any fact indicating a manifest lack of the qualities required by paragraph (1) of Article 14. A party to arbitration proceedings may, in addition, propose the disqualification of an arbitrator on the ground that he was ineligible for appointment to the Tribunal under Section 2 of Chapter IV.

Article 58

The decision on any proposal to disqualify a conciliator or arbitrator shall be taken by the other members of the Commission or Tribunal as the case may be, provided that where those members are equally divided, or in the case of a proposal to disqualify a sole conciliator or arbitrator, or a majority of the conciliators or arbitrators, the Chairman shall take that decision. If it is decided that the proposal is well-founded the conciliator or arbitrator to whom the decision relates shall be replaced in accordance with the provisions of Section 2 of Chapter III or Section 2 of Chapter IV.

Chapter VI

Cost of Proceedings

Article 59

The charges payable by the parties for the use of the facilities of the Centre shall be determined by the Secretary-General in accordance with the regulations adopted by the Administrative Council.

Article 60

(1) Each Commission and each Tribunal shall determine the fees and expenses of its members within limits established from time to time by the Administrative Council and after consultation with the Secretary-General.

(2) Nothing in paragraph (1) of this Article shall preclude the parties from agreeing in advance with the Commission or Tribunal concerned upon the fees and expenses of its members.

Article 61

(1) In the case of conciliation proceedings the fees and expenses of members of the Commission as well as the charges for the use of the facilities of the Centre, shall be borne equally by the parties. Each party shall bear any other expenses it incurs in connection with the proceedings.

(2) In the case of arbitration proceedings the Tribunal shall, except as the parties otherwise agree, assess the expenses incurred by the parties in connection with the proceedings, and shall decide how and by whom those expenses, the fees and expenses of the members of the Tribunal and the charges for the use of the facilities of the Centre shall be paid. Such decision shall form part of the award.

Chapter VII

Place of Proceedings

Article 62

Conciliation and arbitration proceedings shall be held at the seat of the Centre except as hereinafter provided.

Article 63

Conciliation and arbitration proceedings may be held, if the parties so agree,

(a) at the seat of the Permanent Court of Arbitration or of any other appropriate institution, whether private or public, with which the Centre may make arrangements for that purpose; or

(b) at any other place approved by the Commission or Tribunal after consultation with the Secretary-General.

(ii) ICSID Arbitration Rules

RULES OF PROCEDURE FOR ARBITRATION PROCEEDINGS (ARBITRATION RULES) (2006)

I Establishment of the Tribunal

1 General Obligations

2 Method of Constituting the Tribunal in the Absence of Previous Agreement

3 Appointment of Arbitrators to a Tribunal Constituted in Accordance with Convention Article 37(2)(b)

4 Appointment of Arbitrators by the Chairman of the Administrative Council

5 Acceptance of Appointments

6 Constitution of the Tribunal

7 Replacement of Arbitrators

8 Incapacity or Resignation of Arbitrators

9 Disqualification of Arbitrators

10 Procedure during a Vacancy on the Tribunal

11 Filling Vacancies on the Tribunal

12 Resumption of Proceeding after Filling a Vacancy

II Working of the Tribunal

13 Sessions of the Tribunal

14 Sittings of the Tribunal

15 Deliberations of the Tribunal

16 Decisions of the Tribunal

17 Incapacity of the President

18 Representation of the Parties

Annex 2

III General Procedural Provisions

19 Procedural Orders

20 Preliminary Procedural Consultation

21 Pre-Hearing Conference

22 Procedural Languages

23 Copies of Instruments

24 Supporting Documentation

25 Correction of Errors

26 Time Limits

27 Waiver

28 Cost of Proceeding

IV Written and Oral Procedures

29 Normal Procedures

30 Transmission of the Request

31 The Written Procedure

32 The Oral Procedure

33 Marshalling of Evidence

34 Evidence: General Principles

35 Examination of Witnesses and Experts

36 Witnesses and Experts: Special Rules

37 Visits and Inquiries; Submissions of Non-disputing Parties

38 Closure of the Proceeding

V Particular Procedures

39 Provisional Measures

40 Ancillary Claims

41 Preliminary Objections

42 Default

43 Settlement and Discontinuance

44 Discontinuance at Request of a Party

45 Discontinuance for Failure of Parties to Act

VI The Award

46 Preparation of the Award

47 The Award

48 Rendering of the Award

49 Supplementary Decisions and Rectification

VII Interpretation, Revision and Annulment of the Award

50 The Application

51 Interpretation or Revision: Further Procedures

52 Annulment: Further Procedures

53 Rules of Procedure

54 Stay of Enforcement of the Award

55 Resubmission of Dispute after an Annulment

VIII General Provisions

56 Final Provisions

The Rules of Procedure for Arbitration Proceedings (the Arbitration Rules) of ICSID were adopted by the Administrative Council of the Centre pursuant to Article 6(1)(c) of the ICSID Convention.

The Arbitration Rules are supplemented by the Administrative and Financial Regulations of the Centre, in particular by Regulations 14-16, 22-31 and 34(1).

The Arbitration Rules cover the period of time from the disp35h of the notice of registration of a request for arbitration until an award is rendered and all challenges possible to it under the Convention have been exhausted.

The transactions previous to that time are to be regulated in accordance with the Institution Rules.

Arbitration Rules

Chapter I

Establishment of the Tribunal

Rule 1

General Obligations

(1) Upon notification of the registration of the request for arbitration, the parties shall, with all possible dispatch, proceed to constitute a Tribunal, with due regard to Section 2 of Chapter IV of the Convention.

(2) Unless such information is provided in the request, the parties shall communicate to the Secretary-General as soon as possible any provisions agreed by them regarding the number of arbitrators and the method of their appointment.

(3) The majority of the arbitrators shall be nationals of States other than the State party to the dispute and of the State whose national is a party to the dispute, unless the sole arbitrator or each individual member of the Tribunal is appointed by agreement of the parties. Where the Tribunal is to consist of three members, a national of either of these States may not be appointed as an arbitrator by a party without the agreement of the other party to the dispute. Where the Tribunal is to consist of five or more members, nationals of either of these States may not be appointed as arbitrators by a party if appointment by the other party of the same number of arbitrators of either of these nationalities would result in a majority of arbitrators of these nationalities.

(4) No person who had previously acted as a conciliator or arbitrator in any proceeding for the settlement of the dispute may be appointed as a member of the Tribunal.

Rule 2

Method of Constituting the Tribunal in the Absence of Previous Agreement

(1) If the parties, at the time of the registration of the request for arbitration, have not agreed upon the number of arbitrators and the method of their appointment, they shall, unless they agree otherwise, follow the following procedure:

(a) the requesting party shall, within 10 days after the registration of the request, propose to the other party the appointment of a sole arbitrator or of a specified uneven number of arbitrators and specify the method proposed for their appointment;

(b) within 20 days after receipt of the proposals made by the requesting party, the other party shall:

(i) accept such proposals; or

(ii) make other proposals regarding the number of arbitrators and the method of their appointment;

(c) within 20 days after receipt of the reply containing any such other proposals, the requesting party shall notify the other party whether it accepts or rejects such proposals.

(2) The communications provided for in paragraph (1) shall be made or promptly confirmed in writing and shall either be transmitted through the Secretary-General or directly between the parties with a copy to the Secretary-General. The parties shall promptly notify the Secretary-General of the contents of any agreement reached.

(3) At any time 60 days after the registration of the request, if no agreement on another procedure is reached, either party may inform the Secretary-General that it chooses the formula provided for in Article 37(2)(b) of the Convention. The Secretary-General shall thereupon promptly inform the other party that the Tribunal is to be constituted in accordance with that Article.

Rule 3

Appointment of Arbitrators to a Tribunal Constituted in Accordance with Convention Article 37(2)(b)

(1) If the Tribunal is to be constituted in accordance with Article 37(2)(b) of the Convention:

(a) either party shall in a communication to the other party:

(i) name two persons, identifying one of them, who shall not have the same nationality as nor be a national of either party, as the arbitrator appointed by it, and the other as the arbitrator proposed to be the President of the Tribunal; and

(ii) invite the other party to concur in the appointment of the arbitrator proposed to be the President of the Tribunal and to appoint another arbitrator;

(b) promptly upon receipt of this communication the other party shall, in its reply:

(i) name a person as the arbitrator appointed by it, who shall not have the same nationality as nor be a national of either party; and

(ii) concur in the appointment of the arbitrator proposed to be the President of the Tribunal or name another person as the arbitrator proposed to be President;

(c) promptly upon receipt of the reply containing such a proposal, the initiating party shall notify the other party whether it concurs in the appointment of the arbitrator proposed by that party to be the President of the Tribunal.

(2) The communications provided for in this Rule shall be made or promptly confirmed in writing and shall either be transmitted through the Secretary-General or directly between the parties with a copy to the Secretary-General.

Rule 4

Appointment of Arbitrators by the Chairman of the Administrative Council

(1) If the Tribunal is not constituted within 90 days after the dispatch by the Secretary-General of the notice of registration, or such other period as the parties may agree, either party may, through the Secretary-General, address to the Chairman of the Administrative Council a request in writing to appoint the arbitrator or arbitrators not yet appointed and to designate an arbitrator to be the President of the Tribunal.

(2) The provision of paragraph (1) shall apply mutatis mutandis in the event that the parties have agreed that the arbitrators shall elect the President of the Tribunal and they fail to do so.

(3) The Secretary-General shall forthwith send a copy of the request to the other party.

(4) The Chairman shall use his best efforts to comply with that request within 30 days after its receipt. Before he proceeds to make an appointment or designation, with due regard to Articles 38 and 40(1) of the Convention, he shall consult both parties as far as possible.

(5) The Secretary-General shall promptly notify the parties of any appointment or designation made by the Chairman.

Rule 5

Acceptance of Appointments

(1) The party or parties concerned shall notify the Secretary-General of the appointment of each arbitrator and indicate the method of his appointment.

(2) As soon as the Secretary-General has been informed by a party or the Chairman of the Administrative Council of the appointment of an arbitrator, he shall seek an acceptance from the appointee.

(3) If an arbitrator fails to accept his appointment within 15 days, the Secretary-General shall promptly notify the parties,

and if appropriate the Chairman, and invite them to proceed to the appointment of another arbitrator in accordance with the method followed for the previous appointment.

Rule 6

Constitution of the Tribunal

(1) The Tribunal shall be deemed to be constituted and the proceeding to have begun on the date the Secretary-General notifies the parties that all the arbitrators have accepted their appointment.

(2) Before or at the first session of the Tribunal, each arbitrator shall sign a declaration in the following form:

"To the best of my knowledge there is no reason why I should not serve on the Arbitral Tribunal constituted by the International Centre for Settlement of Investment Disputes with respect to a dispute between _____ and_____.

"I shall keep confidential all information coming to my knowledge as a result of my participation in this proceeding, as well as the contents of any award made by the Tribunal.

"I shall judge fairly as between the parties, according to the applicable law, and shall not accept any instruction or compensation with regard to the proceeding from any source except as provided in the Convention on the Settlement of Investment Disputes between States and Nationals of Other States and in the Regulations and Rules made pursuant thereto.

"Attached is a statement of (a) my past and present professional, business and other relationships (if any) with the parties and (b) any other circumstance that might cause my reliability for independent judgment to be questioned by a party. I acknowledge that by signing this declaration, I assume a continuing obligation promptly to notify the Secretary-General of the Centre of any such relationship or circumstance that subsequently arises during this proceeding."

Any arbitrator failing to sign a declaration by the end of the first session of the Tribunal shall be deemed to have resigned.

Rule 7

Replacement of Arbitrators

At any time before the Tribunal is constituted, each party may replace any arbitrator appointed by it and the parties may by common consent agree to replace any arbitrator. The procedure of such replacement shall be in accordance with Rules 1, 5 and 6.

Rule 8

Incapacity or Resignation of Arbitrators

(1) If an arbitrator becomes incapacitated or unable to perform the duties of his office, the procedure in respect of the disqualification of arbitrators set forth in Rule 9 shall apply.

(2) An arbitrator may resign by submitting his resignation to the other members of the Tribunal and the Secretary-General. If the arbitrator was appointed by one of the parties, the Tribunal shall promptly consider the reasons for his resignation and decide whether it consents thereto. The Tribunal shall promptly notify the Secretary-General of its decision.

Rule 9

Disqualification of Arbitrators

(1) A party proposing the disqualification of an arbitrator pursuant to Article 57 of the Convention shall promptly, and in any event before the proceeding is declared closed, file its proposal with the Secretary-General, stating its reasons therefor.

(2) The Secretary-General shall forthwith:

(a) transmit the proposal to the members of the Tribunal and, if it relates to a sole arbitrator or to a majority of the members of the Tribunal, to the Chairman of the Administrative Council; and

(b) notify the other party of the proposal.

(3) The arbitrator to whom the proposal relates may, without delay, furnish explanations to the Tribunal or the Chairman, as the case may be.

(4) Unless the proposal relates to a majority of the members of the Tribunal, the other members shall promptly consider and vote on the proposal in the absence of the arbitrator concerned. If those members are equally divided, they shall, through the Secretary-General, promptly notify the Chairman of the proposal, of any explanation furnished by the arbitrator concerned and of their failure to reach a decision.

(5) Whenever the Chairman has to decide on a proposal to disqualify an arbitrator, he shall use his best efforts to take that decision within 30 days after he has received the proposal.

(6) The proceeding shall be suspended until a decision has been taken on the proposal.

Rule 10

Procedure during a Vacancy on the Tribunal

(1) The Secretary-General shall forthwith notify the parties and, if necessary, the Chairman of the Administrative Council of the disqualification, death, incapacity or resignation of an arbitrator and of the consent, if any, of the Tribunal to a resignation.

(2) Upon the notification by the Secretary-General of a vacancy on the Tribunal, the proceeding shall be or remain suspended until the vacancy has been filled.

Rule 11

Filling Vacancies on the Tribunal

(1) Except as provided in paragraph (2), a vacancy resulting from the disqualification, death, incapacity or resignation of an arbitrator shall be promptly filled by the same method by which his appointment had been made.

(2) In addition to filling vacancies relating to arbitrators appointed by him, the Chairman of the Administrative Council shall appoint a person from the Panel of Arbitrators:

(a) to fill a vacancy caused by the resignation, without the consent of the Tribunal, of an arbitrator appointed by a party; or

(b) at the request of either party, to fill any other vacancy, if no new appointment is made and accepted within 45 days of the notification of the vacancy by the Secretary-General.

(3) The procedure for filling a vacancy shall be in accordance with Rules 1, 4(4), 4(5), 5 and, mutatis mutandis, 6(2).

Rule 12

Resumption of Proceeding after Filling a Vacancy

As soon as a vacancy on the Tribunal has been filled, the proceeding shall continue from the point it had reached at the time the vacancy occurred. The newly appointed arbitrator may, however, require that the oral procedure be recommenced, if this had already been started.

Chapter II

Working of the Tribunal

Rule 13

Sessions of the Tribunal

(1) The Tribunal shall hold its first session within 60 days after its constitution or such other period as the parties may agree. The dates of that session shall be fixed by the President of the Tribunal after consultation with its members and the Secretary-General. If upon its constitution the Tribunal has no President because the parties have agreed that the President shall be elected by its members, the Secretary-General shall fix the dates of that session. In both cases, the parties shall be consulted as far as possible.

(2) The dates of subsequent sessions shall be determined by the Tribunal, after consultation with the Secretary-General and with the parties as far as possible.

(3) The Tribunal shall meet at the seat of the Centre or at such other place as may have been agreed by the parties in accordance with Article 63 of the Convention. If the parties agree that the proceeding shall be held at a place other than the Centre or an institution with which the Centre has made the necessary arrangements, they shall consult with the Secretary-General and request the approval of the Tribunal. Failing such approval, the Tribunal shall meet at the seat of the Centre.

(4) The Secretary-General shall notify the members of the Tribunal and the parties of the dates and place of the sessions of the Tribunal in good time.

Rule 14

Sittings of the Tribunal

(1) The President of the Tribunal shall conduct its hearings and preside at its deliberations.

(2) Except as the parties otherwise agree, the presence of a majority of the members of the Tribunal shall be required at its sittings.

(3) The President of the Tribunal shall fix the date and hour of its sittings.

Rule 15

Deliberations of the Tribunal

(1) The deliberations of the Tribunal shall take place in private and remain secret.

(2) Only members of the Tribunal shall take part in its deliberations. No other person shall be admitted unless the Tribunal decides otherwise.

Rule 16

Decisions of the Tribunal

(1) Decisions of the Tribunal shall be taken by a majority of the votes of all its members. Abstention shall count as a negative vote.

(2) Except as otherwise provided by these Rules or decided by the Tribunal, it may take any decision by correspondence among its members, provided that all of them are consulted. Decisions so taken shall be certified by the President of the Tribunal.

Rule 17

Incapacity of the President

If at any time the President of the Tribunal should be unable to act, his functions shall be performed by one of the other members of the Tribunal, acting in the order in which the Secretary-General had received the notice of their acceptance of their appointment to the Tribunal.

Rule 18

Representation of the Parties

(1) Each party may be represented or assisted by agents, counsel or advocates whose names and authority shall be notified by that party to the Secretary-General, who shall promptly inform the Tribunal and the other party.

(2) For the purposes of these Rules, the expression "party" includes, where the context so admits, an agent, counsel or advocate authorized to represent that party.

Chapter III

General Procedural Provisions

Rule 19

Procedural Orders

The Tribunal shall make the orders required for the conduct of the proceeding.

Rule 20

Preliminary Procedural Consultation

(1) As early as possible after the constitution of a Tribunal, its President shall endeavor to ascertain the views of the parties regarding questions of procedure. For this purpose he may request the parties to meet him. He shall, in particular, seek their views on the following matters:

(a) the number of members of the Tribunal required to constitute a quorum at its sittings;

(b) the language or languages to be used in the proceeding;

(c) the number and sequence of the pleadings and the time limits within which they are to be filed;

(d) the number of copies desired by each party of instruments filed by the other;

(e) dispensing with the written or the oral procedure;

(f) the manner in which the cost of the proceeding is to be apportioned; and

(g) the manner in which the record of the hearings shall be kept.

(2) In the conduct of the proceeding the Tribunal shall apply any agreement between the parties on procedural matters, except as otherwise provided in the Convention or the Administrative and Financial Regulations.

Rule 21

Pre-Hearing Conference

(1) At the request of the Secretary-General or at the discretion of the President of the Tribunal, a pre-hearing conference between the Tribunal and the parties may be held to arrange for an exchange of information and the stipulation of uncontested facts in order to expedite the proceeding.

(2) At the request of the parties, a pre-hearing conference between the Tribunal and the parties, duly represented by their

authorized representatives, may be held to consider the issues in dispute with a view to reaching an amicable settlement.

Rule 22

Procedural Languages

(1) The parties may agree on the use of one or two languages to be used in the proceeding, provided, that, if they agree on any language that is not an official language of the Centre, the Tribunal, after consultation with the Secretary-General, gives its approval. If the parties do not agree on any such procedural language, each of them may select one of the official languages (i.e., English, French and Spanish) for this purpose.

(2) If two procedural languages are selected by the parties, any instrument may be filed in either language. Either language may be used at the hearings, subject, if the Tribunal so requires, to translation and interpretation. The orders and the award of the Tribunal shall be rendered and the record kept in both procedural languages, both versions being equally authentic.

Rule 23

Copies of Instruments

Except as otherwise provided by the Tribunal after consultation with the parties and the Secretary-General, every request, pleading, application, written observation, supporting documentation, if any, or other instrument shall be filed in the form of a signed original accompanied by the following number of additional copies:

(a) before the number of members of the Tribunal has been determined: five;

(b) after the number of members of the Tribunal has been determined: two more than the number of its members.

Rule 24

Supporting Documentation

Supporting documentation shall ordinarily be filed together with the instrument to which it relates, and in any case within the time limit fixed for the filing of such instrument.

Rule 25

Correction of Errors

An accidental error in any instrument or supporting document may, with the consent of the other party or by leave of the Tribunal, be corrected at any time before the award is rendered.

Rule 26

Time Limits

(1) Where required, time limits shall be fixed by the Tribunal by assigning dates for the completion of the various steps in the proceeding. The Tribunal may delegate this power to its President.

(2) The Tribunal may extend any time limit that it has fixed. If the Tribunal is not in session, this power shall be exercised by its President.

(3) Any step taken after expiration of the applicable time limit shall be disregarded unless the Tribunal, in special circumstances and after giving the other party an opportunity of stating its views, decides otherwise.

Rule 27

Waiver

A party which knows or should have known that a provision of the Administrative and Financial Regulations, of these Rules, of any other rules or agreement applicable to the proceeding, or of an order of the Tribunal has not been complied with and which fails to state promptly its objections thereto, shall be deemed — subject to Article 45 of the Convention — to have waived its right to object.

Rule 28

Cost of Proceeding

(1) Without prejudice to the final decision on the payment of the cost of the proceeding, the Tribunal may, unless otherwise agreed by the parties, decide:

(a) at any stage of the proceeding, the portion which each party shall pay, pursuant to Administrative and Financial Regulation 14, of the fees and expenses of the Tribunal and the charges for the use of the facilities of the Centre;

(b) with respect to any part of the proceeding, that the related costs (as determined by the Secretary-General) shall be borne entirely or in a particular share by one of the parties.

(2) Promptly after the closure of the proceeding, each party shall submit to the Tribunal a statement of costs reasonably incurred or borne by it in the proceeding and the Secretary-General shall submit to the Tribunal an account of all amounts paid by each party to the Centre and of all costs incurred by the Centre for the proceeding. The Tribunal may, before the award has been rendered, request the parties and the Secretary-General to provide additional information concerning the cost of the proceeding.

Chapter IV

Written and Oral Procedures

Rule 29

Normal Procedures

Except if the parties otherwise agree, the proceeding shall comprise two distinct phases: a written procedure followed by an oral one.

Rule 30

Transmission of the Request

As soon as the Tribunal is constituted, the Secretary-General shall transmit to each member a copy of the request by which the proceeding was initiated, of the supporting documentation, of the notice of registration and of any communication received from either party in response thereto.

Rule 31

The Written Procedure

(1) In addition to the request for arbitration, the written procedure shall consist of the following pleadings, filed within time limits set by the Tribunal:

(a) a memorial by the requesting party;

(b) a counter-memorial by the other party; and, if the parties so agree or the Tribunal deems it necessary:

(c) a reply by the requesting party; and

(d) a rejoinder by the other party.

(2) If the request was made jointly, each party shall, within the same time limit determined by the Tribunal, file its memorial and, if the parties so agree or the Tribunal deems it necessary, its reply; however, the parties may instead agree that one of them shall, for the purposes of paragraph (1), be considered as the requesting party.

(3) A memorial shall contain: a statement of the relevant facts; a statement of law; and the submissions. A counter-memorial, reply or rejoinder shall contain an admission or denial of the facts stated in the last previous pleading; any additional facts, if necessary; observations concerning the statement of law in the last previous pleading; a statement of law in answer thereto; and the submissions.

Rule 32

The Oral Procedure

(1) The oral procedure shall consist of the hearing by the Tribunal of the parties, their agents, counsel and advocates, and of witnesses and experts.

(2) Unless either party objects, the Tribunal, after consultation with the Secretary-General, may allow other persons, besides the parties, their agents, counsel and advocates, witnesses and experts during their testimony, and officers of the Tribunal, to attend or observe all or part of the hearings, subject to appropriate logistical arrangements. The Tribunal shall for such cases establish procedures for the protection of proprietary or privileged information.

(3) The members of the Tribunal may, during the hearings, put questions to the parties, their agents, counsel and advocates, and ask them for explanations.

Rule 33

Marshalling of Evidence

Without prejudice to the rules concerning the production of documents, each party shall, within time limits fixed by the Tribunal, communicate to the Secretary-General, for transmission to the Tribunal and the other party, precise information regarding the evidence which it intends to produce and that which it intends to request the Tribunal to call for, together with an indication of the points to which such evidence will be directed.

Rule 34

Evidence: General Principles

(1) The Tribunal shall be the judge of the admissibility of any evidence adduced and of its probative value.

(2) The Tribunal may, if it deems it necessary at any stage of the proceeding:

(a) call upon the parties to produce documents, witnesses and experts; and

(b) visit any place connected with the dispute or conduct inquiries there.

(3) The parties shall cooperate with the Tribunal in the production of the evidence and in the other measures provided for in paragraph (2). The Tribunal shall take formal note of the failure of a party to comply with its obligations under this paragraph and of any reasons given for such failure.

(4) Expenses incurred in producing evidence and in taking other measures in accordance with paragraph (2) shall be deemed to constitute part of the expenses incurred by the parties within the meaning of Article 61(2) of the Convention.

Rule 35

Examination of Witnesses and Experts

(1) Witnesses and experts shall be examined before the Tribunal by the parties under the control of its President. Questions may also be put to them by any member of the Tribunal.

(2) Each witness shall make the following declaration before giving his evidence:

"I solemnly declare upon my honour and conscience that I shall speak the truth, the whole truth and nothing but the truth."

(3) Each expert shall make the following declaration before making his statement:

"I solemnly declare upon my honour and conscience that my statement will be in accordance with my sincere belief."

Rule 36

Witnesses and Experts: Special Rules

Notwithstanding Rule 35 the Tribunal may:

(a) admit evidence given by a witness or expert in a written deposition; and

(b) with the consent of both parties, arrange for the examination of a witness or expert otherwise than before the Tribunal itself. The Tribunal shall define the subject of the examination, the time limit, the procedure to be followed and other particulars. The parties may participate in the examination.

Rule 37

Visits and Inquiries; Submissions of Non-disputing Parties

(1) If the Tribunal considers it necessary to visit any place connected with the dispute or to conduct an inquiry there, it shall make an order to this effect. The order shall define the scope of the visit or the subject of the inquiry, the time limit, the procedure to be followed and other particulars. The parties may participate in any visit or inquiry.

(2) After consulting both parties, the Tribunal may allow a person or entity that is not a party to the dispute (in this Rule called the "nondisputing party") to file a written submission with the Tribunal regarding a matter within the scope of the dispute. In determining whether to allow such a filing, the Tribunal shall consider, among other things, the extent to which:

(a) the non-disputing party submission would assist the Tribunal in the determination of a factual or legal issue related to the proceeding by bringing a perspective, particular knowledge or insight that is different from that of the disputing parties;

(b) the non-disputing party submission would address a matter within the scope of the dispute;

(c) the non-disputing party has a significant interest in the proceeding.

The Tribunal shall ensure that the non-disputing party submission does not disrupt the proceeding or unduly burden or unfairly prejudice either party, and that both parties are given an opportunity to present their observations on the non-disputing party submission.

Rule 38

Closure of the Proceeding

(1) When the presentation of the case by the parties is completed, the proceeding shall be declared closed.

(2) Exceptionally, the Tribunal may, before the award has been rendered, reopen the proceeding on the ground that new evidence is forthcoming of such a nature as to constitute a decisive factor, or that there is a vital need for clarification on certain specific points.

Chapter V

Particular Procedures

Rule 39

Provisional Measures

(1) At any time after the institution of the proceeding, a party may request that provisional measures for the preservation of its rights be recommended by the Tribunal. The request shall specify the rights to be preserved, the measures the recommendation of which is requested, and the circumstances that require such measures.

(2) The Tribunal shall give priority to the consideration of a request made pursuant to paragraph (1).

(3) The Tribunal may also recommend provisional measures on its own initiative or recommend measures other than those specified in a request. It may at any time modify or revoke its recommendations.

(4) The Tribunal shall only recommend provisional measures, or modify or revoke its recommendations, after giving each party an opportunity of presenting its observations.

(5) If a party makes a request pursuant to paragraph (1) before the constitution of the Tribunal, the Secretary-General shall, on the application of either party, fix time limits for the parties

to present observations on the request, so that the request and observations may be considered by the Tribunal promptly upon its constitution.

(6) Nothing in this Rule shall prevent the parties, provided that they have so stipulated in the agreement recording their consent, from requesting any judicial or other authority to order provisional measures, prior to or after the institution of the proceeding, for the preservation of their respective rights and interests.

Rule 40

Ancillary Claims

(1) Except as the parties otherwise agree, a party may present an incidental or additional claim or counter-claim arising directly out of the subject-matter of the dispute, provided that such ancillary claim is within the scope of the consent of the parties and is otherwise within the jurisdiction of the Centre.

(2) An incidental or additional claim shall be presented not later than in the reply and a counter-claim no later than in the countermemorial, unless the Tribunal, upon justification by the party presenting the ancillary claim and upon considering any objection of the other party, authorizes the presentation of the claim at a later stage in the proceeding.

(3) The Tribunal shall fix a time limit within which the party against which an ancillary claim is presented may file its observations thereon.

Rule 41

Preliminary Objections

(1) Any objection that the dispute or any ancillary claim is not within the jurisdiction of the Centre or, for other reasons, is not within the competence of the Tribunal shall be made as early as possible. A party shall file the objection with the Secretary-General no later than the expiration of the time limit fixed for the filing of the countermemorial, or, if the objection relates to an ancillary claim, for the filing of the rejoinder—unless the

facts on which the objection is based are unknown to the party at that time.

(2) The Tribunal may on its own initiative consider, at any stage of the proceeding, whether the dispute or any ancillary claim before it is within the jurisdiction of the Centre and within its own competence.

(3) Upon the formal raising of an objection relating to the dispute, the Tribunal may decide to suspend the proceeding on the merits. The President of the Tribunal, after consultation with its other members, shall fix a time limit within which the parties may file observations on the objection.

(4) The Tribunal shall decide whether or not the further procedures relating to the objection made pursuant to paragraph (1) shall be oral. It may deal with the objection as a preliminary question or join it to the merits of the dispute. If the Tribunal overrules the objection or joins it to the merits, it shall once more fix time limits for the further procedures.

(5) Unless the parties have agreed to another expedited procedure for making preliminary objections, a party may, no later than 30 days after the constitution of the Tribunal, and in any event before the first session of the Tribunal, file an objection that a claim is manifestly without legal merit. The party shall specify as precisely as possible the basis for the objection. The Tribunal, after giving the parties the opportunity to present their observations on the objection, shall, at its first session or promptly thereafter, notify the parties of its decision on the objection. The decision of the Tribunal shall be without prejudice to the right of a party to file an objection pursuant to paragraph (1) or to object, in the course of the proceeding, that a claim lacks legal merit.

(6) If the Tribunal decides that the dispute is not within the jurisdiction of the Centre or not within its own competence, or that all claims are manifestly without legal merit, it shall render an award to that effect.

Rule 42

Default

(1) If a party (in this Rule called the "defaulting party") fails to appear or to present its case at any stage of the proceeding, the other party may, at any time prior to the discontinuance of the proceeding, request the Tribunal to deal with the questions submitted to it and to render an award.

(2) The Tribunal shall promptly notify the defaulting party of such a request. Unless it is satisfied that that party does not intend to appear or to present its case in the proceeding, it shall, at the same time, grant a period of grace and to this end:

(a) if that party had failed to file a pleading or any other instrument within the time limit fixed therefor, fix a new time limit for its filing; or

(b) if that party had failed to appear or present its case at a hearing, fix a new date for the hearing.

The period of grace shall not, without the consent of the other party, exceed 60 days.

(3) After the expiration of the period of grace or when, in accordance with paragraph (2), no such period is granted, the Tribunal shall resume the consideration of the dispute. Failure of the defaulting party to appear or to present its case shall not be deemed an admission of the assertions made by the other party.

(4) The Tribunal shall examine the jurisdiction of the Centre and its own competence in the dispute and, if it is satisfied, decide whether the submissions made are well-founded in fact and in law. To this end, it may, at any stage of the proceeding, call on the party appearing to file observations, produce evidence or submit oral explanations.

Rule 43

Settlement and Discontinuance

(1) If, before the award is rendered, the parties agree on a settlement of the dispute or otherwise to discontinue the proceeding, the Tribunal, or the Secretary-General if the Tribunal has not yet been constituted, shall, at their written request, in an order take note of the discontinuance of the proceeding.

(2) If the parties file with the Secretary-General the full and signed text of their settlement and in writing request the Tribunal to embody such settlement in an award, the Tribunal may record the settlement in the form of its award.

Rule 44

Discontinuance at Request of a Party

If a party requests the discontinuance of the proceeding, the Tribunal, or the Secretary-General if the Tribunal has not yet been constituted, shall in an order fix a time limit within which the other party may state whether it opposes the discontinuance. If no objection is made in writing within the time limit, the other party shall be deemed to have acquiesced in the discontinuance and the Tribunal, or if appropriate the Secretary-General, shall in an order take note of the discontinuance of the proceeding. If objection is made, the proceeding shall continue.

Rule 45

Discontinuance for Failure of Parties to Act

If the parties fail to take any steps in the proceeding during six consecutive months or such period as they may agree with the approval of the Tribunal, or of the Secretary-General if the Tribunal has not yet been constituted, they shall be deemed to have discontinued the proceeding and the Tribunal, or if appropriate the Secretary-General, shall, after notice to the parties, in an order take note of the discontinuance.

Chapter VI

The Award

Rule 46

Preparation of the Award

The award (including any individual or dissenting opinion) shall be drawn up and signed within 120 days after closure of the proceeding. The Tribunal may, however, extend this period by a further 60 days if it would otherwise be unable to draw up the award.

Rule 47

The Award

(1) The award shall be in writing and shall contain:

(a) a precise designation of each party;

(b) a statement that the Tribunal was established under the Convention, and a description of the method of its constitution;

(c) the name of each member of the Tribunal, and an identification of the appointing authority of each;

(d) the names of the agents, counsel and advocates of the parties;

(e) the dates and place of the sittings of the Tribunal;

(f) a summary of the proceeding;

(g) a statement of the facts as found by the Tribunal;

(h) the submissions of the parties;

(i) the decision of the Tribunal on every question submitted to it, together with the reasons upon which the decision is based; and

(j) any decision of the Tribunal regarding the cost of the proceeding.

(2) The award shall be signed by the members of the Tribunal who voted for it; the date of each signature shall be indicated.

(3) Any member of the Tribunal may attach his individual opinion to the award, whether he dissents from the majority or not, or a statement of his dissent.

Rule 48

Rendering of the Award

(1) Upon signature by the last arbitrator to sign, the Secretary-General shall promptly:

(a) authenticate the original text of the award and deposit it in the archives of the Centre, together with any individual opinions and statements of dissent; and

(b) dispatch a certified copy of the award (including individual opinions and statements of dissent) to each party, indicating the date of dispatch on the original text and on all copies.

(2) The award shall be deemed to have been rendered on the date on which the certified copies were dispatched.

(3) The Secretary-General shall, upon request, make available to a party additional certified copies of the award.

(4) The Centre shall not publish the award without the consent of the parties. The Centre shall, however, promptly include in its publications excerpts of the legal reasoning of the Tribunal.

Rule 49

Supplementary Decisions and Rectification

(1) Within 45 days after the date on which the award was rendered, either party may request, pursuant to Article 49(2) of the Convention, a supplementary decision on, or the rectification of, the award. Such a request shall be addressed in writing to the Secretary-General. The request shall:

(a) identify the award to which it relates;

(b) indicate the date of the request;

(c) state in detail:

(i) any question which, in the opinion of the requesting party, the Tribunal omitted to decide in the award; and

(ii) any error in the award which the requesting party seeks to have rectified; and

(d) be accompanied by a fee for lodging the request.

(2) Upon receipt of the request and of the lodging fee, the Secretary-General shall forthwith:

(a) register the request;

(b) notify the parties of the registration;

(c) transmit to the other party a copy of the request and of any accompanying documentation; and

(d) transmit to each member of the Tribunal a copy of the notice of registration, together with a copy of the request and of any accompanying documentation.

(3) The President of the Tribunal shall consult the members on whether it is necessary for the Tribunal to meet in order to consider the request. The Tribunal shall fix a time limit for the parties to file their observations on the request and shall determine the procedure for its consideration.

(4) Rules 46-48 shall apply, mutatis mutandis, to any decision of the Tribunal pursuant to this Rule.

(5) If a request is received by the Secretary-General more than 45 days after the award was rendered, he shall refuse to register the request and so inform forthwith the requesting party.

Chapter VII

Interpretation, Revision and Annulment of the Award

Rule 50

The Application

(1) An application for the interpretation, revision or annulment of an award shall be addressed in writing to the Secretary-General and shall:

(a) identify the award to which it relates;

(b) indicate the date of the application;

(c) state in detail:

(i) in an application for interpretation, the precise points in dispute;

(ii) in an application for revision, pursuant to Article 51(1) of the Convention, the change sought in the award, the discovery of some fact of such a nature as decisively to affect the award, and evidence that when the award was rendered that fact was unknown to the Tribunal and to the applicant, and that the applicant's ignorance of that fact was not due to negligence;

(iii) in an application for annulment, pursuant to Article 52(1) of the Convention, the grounds on which it is based. These grounds are limited to the following:

– that the Tribunal was not properly constituted;

– that the Tribunal has manifestly exceeded its powers;

– that there was corruption on the part of a member of the Tribunal;

– that there has been a serious departure from a fundamental rule of procedure;

– that the award has failed to state the reasons on which it is based;

(d) be accompanied by the payment of a fee for lodging the application.

(2) Without prejudice to the provisions of paragraph (3), upon receiving an application and the lodging fee, the Secretary-General shall forthwith:

(a) register the application;

(b) notify the parties of the registration; and

(c) transmit to the other party a copy of the application and of any accompanying documentation.

(3) The Secretary-General shall refuse to register an application for:

(a) revision, if, in accordance with Article 51(2) of the Convention, it is not made within 90 days after the discovery of the new fact and in any event within three years after the date on which the award was rendered (or any subsequent decision or correction);

(b) annulment, if, in accordance with Article 52(2) of the Convention, it is not made:

(i) within 120 days after the date on which the award was rendered (or any subsequent decision or correction) if the application is based on any of the following grounds:

– the Tribunal was not properly constituted;

– the Tribunal has manifestly exceeded its powers;

– there has been a serious departure from a fundamental rule of procedure;

– the award has failed to state the reasons on which it is based;

(ii) in the case of corruption on the part of a member of the Tribunal, within 120 days after discovery thereof, and in any event within three years after the date on which the award was rendered (or any subsequent decision or correction).

(4) If the Secretary-General refuses to register an application for revision, or annulment, he shall forthwith notify the requesting party of his refusal.

Rule 51

Interpretation or Revision: Further Procedures

(1) Upon registration of an application for the interpretation or revision of an award, the Secretary-General shall forthwith:

(a) transmit to each member of the original Tribunal a copy of the notice of registration, together with a copy of the application and of any accompanying documentation; and

(b) request each member of the Tribunal to inform him within a specified time limit whether that member is willing to take part in the consideration of the application.

(2) If all members of the Tribunal express their willingness to take part in the consideration of the application, the Secretary-General shall so notify the members of the Tribunal and the parties. Upon dispatch of these notices the Tribunal shall be deemed to be reconstituted.

(3) If the Tribunal cannot be reconstituted in accordance with paragraph (2), the Secretary-General shall so notify the parties and invite them to proceed, as soon as possible, to constitute a new Tribunal, including the same number of arbitrators, and appointed by the same method, as the original one.

Rule 52

Annulment: Further Procedures

(1) Upon registration of an application for the annulment of an award, the Secretary-General shall forthwith request the Chairman of the Administrative Council to appoint an ad hoc Committee in accordance with Article 52(3) of the Convention.

(2) The Committee shall be deemed to be constituted on the date the Secretary-General notifies the parties that all members have accepted their appointment. Before or at the first session of the Committee, each member shall sign a declaration conforming to that set forth in Rule 6(2).

Rule 53

Rules of Procedure

The provisions of these Rules shall apply mutatis mutandis to any procedure relating to the interpretation, revision or annulment of an award and to the decision of the Tribunal or Committee.

Rule 54

Stay of Enforcement of the Award

(1) The party applying for the interpretation, revision or annulment of an award may in its application, and either party may at any time before the final disposition of the application, request a stay in the enforcement of part or all of the award to which the application relates. The Tribunal or Committee shall give priority to the consideration of such a request.

(2) If an application for the revision or annulment of an award contains a request for a stay of its enforcement, the Secretary-General shall, together with the notice of registration, inform both parties of the provisional stay of the award. As soon as the Tribunal or Committee is constituted it shall, if either party requests, rule within 30 days on whether such stay should be continued; unless it decides to continue the stay, it shall automatically be terminated.

(3) If a stay of enforcement has been granted pursuant to paragraph (1) or continued pursuant to paragraph (2), the Tribunal or Committee may at any time modify or terminate the stay at the request of either party. All stays shall automatically terminate on the date on which a final decision is rendered on the application, except that a Committee granting the partial annulment of an award may order the temporary stay of enforcement of the unannulled portion in order to give either party an opportunity to request any new Tribunal constituted pursuant to Article 52(6) of the Convention to grant a stay pursuant to Rule 55(3).

163

(4) A request pursuant to paragraph (1), (2) (second sentence) or (3) shall specify the circumstances that require the stay or its modification or termination. A request shall only be granted after the Tribunal or Committee has given each party an opportunity of presenting is observations.

(5) The Secretary-General shall promptly notify both parties of the stay of enforcement of any award and of the modification or termination of such a stay, which shall become effective on the date on which he dispatches such notification.

Rule 55

Resubmission of Dispute after an Annulment

(1) If a Committee annuls part or all of an award, either party may request the resubmission of the dispute to a new Tribunal. Such a request shall be addressed in writing to the Secretary-General and shall:

(a) identify the award to which it relates;

(b) indicate the date of the request;

(c) explain in detail what aspect of the dispute is to be submitted to the Tribunal; and

(d) be accompanied by a fee for lodging the request.

(2) Upon receipt of the request and of the lodging fee, the Secretary-General shall forthwith:

(a) register it in the Arbitration Register;

(b) notify both parties of the registration;

(c) transmit to the other party a copy of the request and of any accompanying documentation; and

(d) invite the parties to proceed, as soon as possible, to constitute a new Tribunal, including the same number of arbitrators, and appointed by the same method, as the original one.

(3) If the original award had only been annulled in part, the new Tribunal shall not reconsider any portion of the award not so annulled. It may, however, in accordance with the procedures

set forth in Rule 54, stay or continue to stay the enforcement of the unannulled portion of the award until the date its own award is rendered.

(4) Except as otherwise provided in paragraphs (1)–(3), these Rules shall apply to a proceeding on a resubmitted dispute in the same manner as if such dispute had been submitted pursuant to the Institution Rules.

Chapter VIII

General Provisions

Rule 56

Final Provisions

(1) The texts of these Rules in each official language of the Centre shall be equally authentic.

(2) These Rules may be cited as the "Arbitration Rules" of the Centre.

(iii) ICSID Enforcement Act (England and Wales)

ARBITRATION (INTERNATIONAL INVESTMENT DISPUTES) ACT 1966

An Act to implement an international Convention on the settlement of investment disputes between States and nationals of other States.

[13th December 1966]

1.— Registration of Convention awards.

(1) This section has effect as respects awards rendered pursuant to the Convention on the settlement of investment disputes between States and nationals of other States which was opened for signature in Washington on 18th March 1965.

That Convention is in this Act called "the Convention", and its text is set out in the Schedule to this Act.

(2) A person seeking recognition or enforcement of such an award shall be entitled to have the award registered in the High Court subject to proof of the prescribed matters and to the other provisions of this Act.

(4) In addition to the pecuniary obligations imposed by the award, the award shall be registered for the reasonable costs of and incidental to registration.

(5) If at the date of the application for registration the pecuniary obligations imposed by the award have been partly satisfied, the award shall be registered only in respect of the balance, and accordingly if those obligations have then been wholly satisfied, the award shall not be registered.

(6) The power to make rules of court under section 84 of the Senior Courts Act 1981 shall include power—

(a) to prescribe the procedure for applying for registration under this section, and to require an applicant to give prior notice of his intention to other parties,

(b) to prescribe the matters to be proved on the application and the manner of proof, and in particular to require the applicant to furnish a copy of the award certified pursuant to the Convention,

(c) to provide for the service of notice of registration of the award by the applicant on other parties,

and in this and the next following section "prescribed" means prescribed by rules of court.

(7) For the purposes of this and the next following section —

(a) "award"shall include any decision interpreting, revising or annulling an award, being a decision pursuant to the Convention, and any decision as to costs which under the Convention is to form part of the award,

(b) an award shall be deemed to have been rendered pursuant to the Convention on the date on which certified copies of the award were pursuant to the Convention dispatched to the parties.

(8) This and the next following section shall bind the Crown (but not so as to make an award enforceable against the Crown in a manner in which a judgment would not be enforceable against the Crown).

2.— Effect of registration.

(1) Subject to the provisions of this Act, an award registered under section 1 above shall, as respects the pecuniary obligations which it imposes, be of the same force and effect for the purposes of execution as if it had been a judgment of the High Court given when the award was rendered pursuant to the Convention and entered on the date of registration under this Act, and, so far as relates to such pecuniary obligations —

(a) proceedings may be taken on the award,

(b) the sum for which the award is registered shall carry interest,

(c) the High Court shall have the same control over the execution of the award, as if the award had been such a judgment of the High Court.

(2) Rules of court under section 84 of the Supreme Court Act 1981 may contain provisions requiring the court on proof of the prescribed matters to stay execution of any award registered under this Act so as to take account of cases where enforcement of the award has been stayed (whether provisionally or otherwise) pursuant to the Convention, and may provide for the provisional stay of execution of the award where an application is made pursuant to the Convention which, if granted, might result in a stay of enforcement of the award.

3.— Application of provisions of Arbitration Act 1996.

(1) The Lord Chancellor may by order direct that any of the provisions contained in section 36 and 38 to 44 of the Arbitration Act 1996 (provisions concerning the conduct of arbitral proceedings, etc.) shall apply to such proceedings pursuant to the Convention as are specified in the order with or without any modifications or exceptions specified in the order.

(2) Subject to subsection (1), the Arbitration Act 1996 shall not apply to proceedings pursuant to the Convention, but this subsection shall not be taken as affecting section 9 of that Act (stay of legal proceedings in respect of matter subject to arbitration).

(3) An order made under this section—

(a) may be varied or revoked by a subsequent order so made, and

(b) shall be contained in a statutory instrument.

4.— Status, immunities and privileges conferred by the Convention.

(1) In Section 6 of Chapter I of the Convention (which governs the status, immunities and privileges of the International Centre for Settlement of Investment Disputes established by the Convention, of members of its Council and Secretariat and of persons concerned with conciliation or arbitration under the Convention) Articles 18 to 20, Article 21(a) (with Article 22 as

168

it applies Article 21(a)), Article 23(1) and Article 24 shall have the force of law.

(2) Nothing in Article 24(1) of the Convention as given the force of law by this section shall be construed as—

(a) entitling the said Centre to import goods free of customs duty without any restriction on their subsequent sale in the country to which they were imported, or

(b) conferring on that Centre any exemption from duties or taxes which form part of the price of goods sold, or

(c) conferring on that Centre any exemption from duties or taxes which are no more than charges for services rendered.

(3) For the purposes of Article 20 and Article 21(a) of the Convention as given the force of law by this section, a statement to the effect that the said Centre has waived an immunity in the circumstances specified in the statement, being a statement certified by the Secretary-General of the said Centre (or by the person acting as Secretary-General), shall be conclusive evidence.

5.— Government contribution to expenses under the Convention.

The Treasury may discharge any obligations of Her Majesty's Government in the United Kingdom arising under Article 17 of the Convention (which obliges the Contracting States to meet any deficit of the International Centre for Settlement of Investment Disputes established under the Convention), and any sums required for that purpose shall be met out of money provided by Parliament.

(iv) Code of Conduct for Litigation Funders (January 2014)

1. This code ('the Code') sets out standards of practice and behaviour to be observed by Funders (as defined in clause 2 below) who are Members of The Association of Litigation Funders of England & Wales ('the Association') in respect of funding the resolution of disputes within England and Wales.

2. A litigation funder:

    2.1 has access to funds immediately within its control, including within a corporate parent or subsidiary ('Funder's Subsidiary'); or

    2.2 acts as the exclusive investment advisor to an entity or entities having access to funds immediately within its or their control, including within a corporate parent or subsidiary ('Associated Entity'),

    ('a Funder') in each case:

    2.3 to fund the resolution of disputes within England and Wales; and

    2.4 where the funds are invested pursuant to a Litigation Funding Agreement ('LFA') to enable a party to a dispute ('the Funded Party') to meet the costs (including pre-action costs) of resolving disputes by litigation, arbitration or other dispute resolution procedures.

    In return the Funder, Funder's Subsidiary or Associated Entity:

    2.5 receives a share of the proceeds if the claim is successful (as defined in the LFA); and

    2.6 does not seek any payment from the Funded Party in excess of the amount of the proceeds of the dispute that is being funded, unless the Funded Party is in material breach of the provisions of the LFA.

3. A Funder shall be deemed to have adopted the Code in respect of funding the resolution of disputes within England and Wales.

4. A Funder shall accept responsibility to the Association for compliance with the Code by a Funder's Subsidiary or Associated Entity. By so doing a Funder shall not accept legal responsibility to a Funded Party, which shall be a matter governed, if at all, by the provisions of the LFA.

5. A Funder shall inform a Funded Party as soon as possible and prior to execution of an LFA:

    5.1 if the Funder is acting for and/or on behalf of a Funder's Subsidiary or an Associated Entity in respect of funding the resolution of disputes within England & Wales; and

    5.2 whether the LFA will be entered into by the Funder, a Funder's Subsidiary or an Associated Entity.

6. The promotional literature of a Funder must be clear and not misleading.

7. A Funder will observe the confidentiality of all information and documentation relating to the dispute to the extent that the law permits, and subject to the terms of any Confidentiality or Non-Disclosure Agreement agreed between the Funder and the Funded Party. For the avoidance of doubt, the Funder is responsible for the purposes of this Code for preserving confidentiality on behalf of any Funder's Subsidiary or Associated Entity.

8. An LFA is a contractually binding agreement entered into between a Funder, a Funder's Subsidiary or Associated Entity and a Funded Party relating to the resolution of disputes within England and Wales.

9. A Funder will:

    9.1 take reasonable steps to ensure that the Funded Party shall have received independent advice on the terms of the LFA prior to its execution, which obligation shall be satisfied if the Funded Party confirms in writing to the

Funder that the Funded Party has taken advice from the solicitor or barrister instructed in the dispute;

9.2 not take any steps that cause or are likely to cause the Funded Party's solicitor or barrister to act in breach of their professional duties;

9.3 not seek to influence the Funded Party's solicitor or barrister to cede control or conduct of the dispute to the Funder;

9.4 Maintain at all times access to adequate financial resources to meet the obligations of the Funder, its Funder Subsidiaries and Associated Entities to fund all the disputes that they have agreed to fund and in particular will;

9.4.1 ensure that the Funder, its Funder Subsidiaries and Associated Entities maintain the capacity;

9.4.1.1. to pay all debts when they become due and payable; and

9.4.1.2. to cover aggregate funding liabilities under all of their LFAs for a minimum period of 36 months.

9.4.2 maintain access to a minimum of £2m of capital or such other amount as stipulated by the Association;

9.4.3 accept a continuous disclosure obligation in respect of its capital adequacy, including a specific obligation to notify timeously the Association and the Funded Party if the Funder reasonably believes that its representations in respect of capital adequacy under the Code are no longer valid because of changed circumstances;

9.4.4 undertake that it will be audited annually by a recognised national or international audit firm and shall provide the Association with:

9.4.4.1. a copy of the audit opinion given by the audit firm on the Funder's or Funder's Subsidiary's most recent annual financial statements (but not the underlying financial statements), or in the case of Funders who are investment advisors to an Associated Entity, the audit opinion given by the audit firm in respect of the Associated Entity (but not the underlying financial statements), within one month of receipt of the opinion and in any case within six months of each fiscal year end. If the audit opinion provided is qualified (except as to any emphasis of matters relating to the uncertainty of valuing relevant litigation funding investments) or expresses any question as to the ability of the firm to continue as a going concern, the Association shall be entitled to enquire further into the qualification expressed and take any further action it deems appropriate; and

9.4.4.2. reasonable evidence from a qualified third party (preferably from an auditor, but alternatively from a third party administrator or bank) that the Funder or Funder's Subsidiary or Associated Entity satisfies the minimum capital requirement prevailing at the time of annual subscription.

9.5 comply with the Rules of the Association as to capital adequacy as amended from time to time.

10. The LFA shall state whether (and if so to what extent) the Funder or Funder's Subsidiary or Associated Party is liable to the Funded Party to:

10.1 meet any liability for adverse costs;

10.2 pay any premium (including insurance premium tax) to obtain costs insurance;

10.3 provide security for costs; and

10.4 meet any other financial liability.

11. The LFA shall state whether (and if so how) the Funder or Funder's Subsidiary or Associated Entity may:

11.1 provide input to the Funder Party's decisions in relation to settlements;

11.2 terminate the LFA in the event that the Funder or Funder's Subsidiary or Associated Entity:

11.2.1 reasonably ceases to be satisfied about the merits of the dispute;

11.2.2 reasonably believes that the dispute is no longer commercially viable; or

11.2.3 reasonably believes that there has been a material breach of the LFA by the Funded Party.

12. The LFA shall not establish a discretionary right for a Funder or Funder's Subsidiary or Associated Party to terminate a LFA in the absence of the circumstances described in clause 11.2.

13. If the LFA does give the Funder or Funder's Subsidiary or Associated Entity any of the rights described in clause 11, the LFA shall provide that:

13.1 if the Funder or Funder's Subsidiary or Associated Entity terminates the LFA, the Funder or Funder's Subsidiary or Associated Entity shall remain liable for all funding obligations accrued to the date of termination unless the termination is due to a material breach under clause 11.2.3;

13.2 if there is a dispute between the Funder, Funder's Subsidiary or Associated Entity and the Funded Party about settlement or about termination of the LFA, a binding opinion shall be obtained from a Queen's Counsel who shall be instructed jointly or nominated by the Chairman of the Bar Council.

14. Breach by the Funder's Subsidiary or Associated Entity of the provisions of the Code shall constitute a breach of the Code by the Funder.

15. The Association shall maintain a complaints procedure. A Funder consents to the complaints procedure as it may be varied

from time to time in respect of any relevant act or omission by the Funder, Funder's Subsidiary or Associated Entity.

16. The Code (as amended) applies to LFAs commencing on or after the date hereof.

14th January 2014

ANNEX 3: Recent BIT Arbitration Decisions Which Impact Upon Key Concepts

The cases below cover the following issues, and are current as at August 2015.

1. Definition of Investor;

2. Definition of Investment;

3. Fair and Equitable Treatment;

4. Full protection and security;

5. Expropriation;

6. Umbrella clauses;

7. MFN clauses;

8. Denial of justice; and

9. Quantification.

1. INVESTOR

Case	Date	Summary
Alps Finance and Trade AG v Slovak Republic **UNCITRAL**	Award: 5 March 2011	Tribunal declined jurisdiction on the grounds that the claimant was not an "investor", and the claimant's business was not an "investment
Libananco Holdings Co. Limited v. Republic of Turkey **(ICSID Case No. ARB/06/8)**	Award: 2 September 2011; Decision on Applicant's Request for a Continued Stay of Enforcement of the Award – 7 May 2012	The tribunal declined jurisdiction on the grounds that the claimant was not an "investor" under the ECT, due to its failure to show that it owned the businesses at issue at the time of the alleged expropriation.
Pac Rim Cayman LLC v. The Republic of El Salvador **(ICSID Case No. ARB/09/12)**	Decision on the Respondent's Jurisdictional Objections: 1 June 2012	Discusses change of nationality, and whether and when it becomes an abuse of process.
Standard Chartered Bank v. The United Republic of Tanzania **(ICSID Case No. ARB/10/12)**	Award: 2 November 2012.	Investment must have been made at claimant's direction, funded by him and actively controlled by him for him to be regards as an investor.
KT Asia Investment Group B.V. v Republic of Kazakhstan **(ICSID Case No. ARB/09/8)**	Award, 17 October 2013	If a Claimant was an investor within the terms of the relevant BIT, which provided that a legal entity constituted under the laws of one country was an investor, without the need for any further requirements, then no further requirements (ie, need for real and effective control) could be added.

Case	Date	Summary
ConocoPhillips Petrozuata B.V. and Ors. v Bolivian Republic of Venezuela (ICSID Case No. ARB/07/30)	Decision on Jurisdiction and Merits, 3 September 2013	A tribunal may reject a respondent's argument that a claimant company is a "corporation of convenience" created for the sole purpose of gaining access to ICSID – in this case, the restructuring at issue had been carried out before any claims had been made or were a prospect (contrast this with Tidewater Inc. et al v. The Bolivarian Republic of Venezuela (ICSID Case No. ARB/10/5), Decision on Jurisdiction, 8 February 2013 - restructuring investments only in order to gain jurisdiction under a BIT may result in a denial of jurisdiction where it constitutes abuse).
National Gas SAE v Arab Republic of Egypt, ICSID Case No. ARB/11/7	Decision, 3 April 2014	Tribunal declined jurisdiction. In the present case, notwithstanding that Mr Ginena, an Egyptian-Canadian dual national, had chosen his corporate structure for legitimate fiscal reasons and not as an exercise in forum shopping, the corporations which owned the shares in the Claimant were mere shell companies masking the fact that Mr Ginena was the Claimant's true controller, therefore the Claimant was not under "foreign control" and the Tribunal did not have jurisdiction over the Claimant.

Annex 3

2. INVESTMENT

Alpha Projektholding GmbH v. Ukraine **(ICSID Case No. ARB/07/16)**	Award – 8 November 2010	Tribunal found that it did have jurisdiction (after discussing BIT and ICSID Convention definitions of jurisdiction). It is the character of the project in toto which determines the nature of the commercial arrangements and not the individual agreements in isolation.
CEMEX Caracas Investments B.V. and CEMEX Caracas II Investments B.V. v. Bolivarian Republic of Venezuela,(ICSID Case No. ARB/08/15)	Decision: 30 December 2010	The tribunal affirmed that the BIT in this case covered indirect investments and entitled the claimants to assert their claims for alleged treaty violations.
Malicorp v Egypt **(ICSID Case No. ARB/08/18)**	Decision: 7 February 2011	Jurisdiction accepted. In order for a proceeding based on breach of a treaty to be admissible, the investment to which the dispute relates must pass a double test (also known as the "double keyhole approach" or "double-barrelled test"- it must in practice correspond: - on the one hand, to the meaning given to the term by the treaty, which defines the framework of the consent given by the State, and also - on the other, to the meaning given in the ICSID Convention, which determines the jurisdiction of the Centre and the arbitral tribunals acting under its auspices. Costs incurred during negotiations with a view to concluding a contract do not constitute an investment if in the end the State finally refuses to sign it.

180

GEA v Ukraine **(ICSID Case No. ARB/08/16)**	Award: 31 March 2011	An arbitral award concerning contractual rights and obligations does not constitute an investment. In order for the Tribunal to hear the Claimant's claims, the Claimant must have held an interest in the alleged investment before the alleged treaty violations were committed.
HICEE v. Slovak Republic **PCA 2009-11**	Partial Award: 23 May 2011	The tribunal found under the BIT, there was no protection for investments made by a locally incorporated entity in other locally incorporated entities.
White Industries Australia Ltd v India **UNCITRAL**	Award: 30 November 2011	Tribunal did have jurisdiction over the dispute – the arbitration award at issue arose from a long-term contract between the parties, and was protected as a "continuation or transformation of the original investment".
Chevron Corporation and Texaco Petroleum Corporation v. The Republic of Ecuador **(UNCITRAL, PCA Case No. 2009-23),**	Third interim award on jurisdiction and admissibility: 27 February 2012	The tribunal rejected jurisdictional challenges by Ecuador, and in particular, held that the settlement agreement and concession agreement must be viewed as a single arrangement.
Caratube International Oil Company LLP v. The Republic of Kazakhstan **(ICSID Case No. ARB/08/12),**	Award, 5 June 2012	Investment requires a contribution to be made and that it involves some degree of risk.
Daimler Financial Services AG v. Argentine Republic **(ICSID Case No. ARB/05/1)**	Award, 22 August 2012	Claims in principle separable from underlying investment. Any qualifying investor who suffered damages can claim.
Quiborax S.A., Non Metallic Minerals S.A. and Allan Fosk Kaplún v. Plurinational State of Bolivia **(ICSID Case No. ARB/06/2),**	Decision on Jurisdiction, 27 September 2012	Distinction between object of investment and action of investing.

181

Deutsche Bank AG v. Democratic Socialist Republic of Sri Lanka (ICSID Case No. ARB/09/2)	Award, 31 October 2012	Regularity of profit and return not necessarily a definitional bench-mark.
Electrabel S.A. v. Republic of Hungary (ICSID Case No. ARB/07/19)	Decision on Jurisdiction, Applicable Law and Liability, 30 November 2012	Definitional criteria – a contribution; a certain duration; and an element of risk.
KT Asia Investment Group B.V. v Republic of Kazakhstan (ICSID Case No. ARB/09/8)	Award, 17 October 2013	Factors that may suggest that there is no investment include no contribution in relation to the investment (or evidence of ability to make such an investment in future); that the claimant had no funds of significance, other than a small amount to pay administrative expenses; the purchase of the investment at an undervalue and failure to actually pay for the shares; absence of risk, particularly where payment for the investment was made by way of loans, no security was given for those loans, and eventually the loans were written off and the lenders liquidated; and the intended short duration of the investment (even if circumstances – in the present case the financial crisis – meant that the shares were in fact held longer than intended).

Ambiente Ufficio S.p.A. and others v. Argentine Republic (formerly Giordano Alpi and others v. Argentine Republic) (ICSID Case No. ARB/08/9)	Decision on Jurisdiction and Admissibility, 8 February 2013	Considering the territoriality requirement of the relevant bilateral investment treaty and how that applied to the investment at issue (sovereign bond instruments issued by Argentina and sold in the international markets, and security entitlements which had been purchased in the Italian market), a majority of the tribunal dismissed Argentina's argument that the investment was not made "in the territory" of the respondent as required by the BIT. The tribunal found that "looking at the investment operation at stake as a whole and in terms of its economic realities, it is hard to imagine the investment's situs to be elsewhere than in Argentina." Instruments such as sovereign bonds did not compare to a "single commercial transaction", and should be protected if and to the extent that the contracting parties to the BIT intended those investments to be protected.
Philip Morris Brands Sàrl, Philip Morris Products S.A. and Abal Hermanos S.A. v. Oriental Republic of Uruguay (ICSID Case No. ARB/10/7)	Decision on Jurisdiction, 2 July 2013	The definition of investment "covers a wide range of economic operations confirming the broad scope of its application", although States have the ability to restrict the definition of "investment" in treaties.
Metal-Tech Ltd. v. Republic of Uzbekistan, ICSID Case No. ARB/10/3	Award, 4 October 2013	Compliance with the laws of the host State and good faith are not elements of an objective definition of "investment", but States may choose to limit treaty protection to investments made in accordance with the laws of the host State. In the present case, "implemented in accordance with the laws and regulations" only required the investment to comply with local laws at the time of establishment (jurisdiction was denied in that case as the claimant had made payments to officials at the relevant time in breach of national anti-corruption laws).

Annex 3

3. FAIR AND EQUITABLE TREATMENT

Case	Date	Summary
AES Summit Generation Limited and AES-Tisza Erömü Kft. v. Hungary (ICSID Case No ARB/07/22)	Award: 23 September 2010	Claimant failed in its claims of fair and equitable treatment. Legitimate expectations can only be created at the moment of the investment. It is not every process failing or imperfection that will amount to a failure to provide fair and equitable treatment. The standard is not one of perfection. It is only when a state's acts or procedural omissions are, on the facts and in the context before the adjudicator, manifestly unfair or unreasonable (such as would shock, or at least surprise a sense of juridical propriety) – to use the words of the Tecmed Tribunal – that the standard can be said to have been infringed.
RSM Production Corporation and others v. Grenada (ICSID Case No ARB/10/6)	Award: 10 December 2010	The tribunal dismissed the investor's claims as 'manifestly without legal merit' pursuant to ICSID Arbitration Rule 41(5), on the grounds that the legal and factual bases on which the investor's claims depended had already been fully litigated in a prior contractual arbitration

Case	Date	Summary
Paushok v Mongolia	Award: 28 April 2011	There had been no breach of the obligation for fair and equitable treatment, and no expropriation. The fact that a democratically elected legislature has passed legislation that may be considered as ill-conceived, counter-productive and excessively burdensome does not automatically allow to conclude that a breach of an investment treaty has occurred. An investor has to be aware that modifications of taxation levels represent a risk for his or her investment; without a stabilization agreement, he or she cannot establish a legitimate expectation that a state will refrain from increasing taxes.
El Paso v Argentina **(ICSID Case No ARB/03/15)**	Award: 31 October 2011	The tribunal found that none of the individual measures constituted a breach of the FET clause; but the cumulative effect of those measures constituted a breach of the FET clause as it was a total alteration of the entire legal setup for foreign investments in violation of a special commitment of Argentina that such a total alteration would not take place.
Spyridon Roussalis v. Romania **(ICSID Case No. ARB/06/1)**	Award: 7 December 2011	No case of breach of the obligation of fair and equitable treatment was made out. The majority found that the tribunal did not have jurisdiction over the respondent's counter-claim, on the basis that the consent clause in the underlying treaty limited jurisdiction to claims brought by investors about obligations of the host State

Case	Date	Summary
Toto Costruzioni Generali S.p.A. v. Republic of Lebanon **(ICSID Case No ARB/07/12)**	Award: 7 June 2012	Lebanon had not breached its obligations to be fair and equitable. An investor has to be aware that modifications of taxation levels represent a risk for his or her investment; without a stabilization agreement, he or she cannot establish a legitimate expectation that a state will refrain from increasing taxes.
Swisslion DOO Skopje v. Macedonia, former Yugoslav Republic of **(ICSID Case No. ARB/09/16)**	Award: 6 July, 2012	Proceedings against the Claimant did not breach the BIT but measures "on the margins" of the proceedings did
Ulysseas Inc. v Ecuador	12 June 2012	The tribunal held that the respondent had not breached any of its obligations under the BIT in relation to the claimant's investment, and dismissed all of the claimant's claims. Full protection and security is a standard of treatment other than fair and equitable treatment.
Occidental Petroleum Corporation and Occidental Exploration and Production Company v. The Republic of Ecuador **(ICSID Case No ARB/06/11)**	Award: 5 October 2012	The Tribunal found that Ecuador had acted in breach of the Ecuador/US BIT by failing to accord fair and equitable treatment to Occidental's investment, a breach that was tantamount to expropriation. Ecuador had passed a decree terminating a contract with Occidental in breach of both Ecuadorian and customary international law. Also considered the standard of proportionality.
Bosh International, Inc and B&P Ltd Foreign Investments Enterprise v. Ukraine **(ICSID Case No. ARB/08/11)**	Award, 25 October 2012	State needs to violate a "certain threshold of propriety".

Case	Date	Summary
Deutsche Bank AG v. Democratic Socialist Republic of Sri Lanka **(ICSID Case No. ARB/09/2)**	Award: 31 October 2012	Not materially different from the standard of treatment in customary international law.
Electrabel S.A. v. Republic of Hungary **(ICSID Case No. ARB/07/19),**	Decision on Jurisdiction, Applicable Law and Liability, 30 November 2012	State entitled to maintain a degree of regulatory flexibility to respond to changing circumstances in the public interest.
Franck Charles Arif v. Moldova **(ICSID Case No ARB/11/23)**	Award: 8 April 2013	The Tribunal found that Moldova breached the fair and equitable treatment standard of the BIT in relation to Mr. Arif's investment in the Airport. Moldova was therefore ordered to restitute Claimant's investment in the Airport store, or, if restitution is not provided within 60 days or if Moldova's proposal for restitution is refused by Mr. Arif, who has a discretionary power to reject it, Moldova will have to pay Mr. Arif damages in the amount of 35,136,294 MDL, plus interest at a rate of EURIBOR.
Inmaris Perestroika Sailing Maritime Services GmbH and Others v. Ukraine **(ICSID Case No ARB/08/8)**	Award: 1 May 2013	The Tribunal found in favour of the Claimants on all matters. Ukraine had breached its obligations of fair and equitable treatment under Article 2(1) of the BIT
Rompetrol v Romania **(ICSID Case No ARB/06/3)**	Award: 6 May 2013	The Tribunal dismissed all the claims apart from a claim for breach of the "fair and equitable treatment" requirement laid down in Article 3(1) of the BIT. Tribunal determined that a breach pursuant to the "cumulative effect of individual acts of a less severe kind had taken place. The Claimant had not met the onus of proving that it had suffered economic loss or damage as a result of this breach, however, and so its claim for damages, including moral/reputation damages, was dismissed.

Annex 3

Case	Date	Summary
Micula et al v. Romania (ICSID Case No. ARB/05/20)	Award, 11 December 2013	The respondent's conduct does not need to be egregious to amount to a violation of the "fair and equitable treatment" standard, and such a clause should not be seen as equivalent to a stabilisation clause – the state's conduct will not contravene the standard where an investor's legitimate expectations are protected and the respondent's conduct is substantially and procedurally proper. Conduct that would violate the "fair and equitable treatment" standard includes that which is substantially improper (for example, conduct that is arbitrary, manifestly unreasonable, discriminatory or in bad faith). Transparency and consistency duties arising out of the "fair and equitable treatment" standard should be based on the circumstances in each case.
Renée Rose Levy de Levi v. Republic of Peru (ICSID Case No. ARB/10/17)	Award, 26 February 2014	The legitimate expectations of an investor are linked to the standard of fair and equitable treatment. For an investor to make a decision on an investment, an important element usually considered is the stability of the country's legal system, although this does not mean a freezing of the legal system or making it impossible for the State to reform laws and other regulations in force at the time the investor made the investment.

Case	Date	Summary
Gold Reserve Inc. v. Bolivarian Republic of Venezuela (ICSID Case No. ARB(AF)/09/1)	Award, 22 September 2014	Even if a measure or conduct by the State, taken in isolation, does not rise to the level of a breach of the FET, such a breach may result from a series of circumstances or a combination of measures, particularly where the measures are part of a State policy aimed at gaining control of the object of the investment. The investor's legitimate expectations are a central consideration in the analysis of whether treatment was fair and equitable in the circumstances. Legitimate expectations are based on undertakings and representations made explicitly or implicitly by the host State and are created when a State's conduct is such that an investor may reasonably rely on that conduct as being consistent. A reversal of assurances by the host State that have led to legitimate expectations will violate the principle of fair and equitable treatment.

Annex 3

4. FULL PROTECTION AND SECURITY

Case	Date	Summary
Gold Reserve Inc. v. Bolivarian Republic of Venezuela (ICSID Case No. ARB(AF)/09/1)	Award, 22 September 2014	Tribunal dismissed Gold Reserve's claim under Article II(2) of the BIT (providing for the duty to accord full protection and security to investments). While some investment treaty tribunals have extended the concept of full protection and security to an obligation to provide regulatory and legal protections, the more traditional, and commonly accepted view is that this standard of treatment refers to protection against physical harm to persons and property. There was no suggestion in the present case that Venezuela failed to protect Gold Reserve's investment from physical harm, and therefore no breach of the full protection and security standard occurred.

5. EXPROPRIATION

Case	Date	Summary
AES Summit Generation Limited and AES-Tisza Erömü Kft. v. Hungary (ICSID Case No ARB/07/22)	Award: 23 September 2010	No expropriation. For an expropriation to occur, it is necessary for the investor to be deprived, in whole or significant part, of the property in or effective control of its investment: or for its investment to be deprived, in whole or significant part, of its value.
El Paso v Argentina (ICSID Case No ARB/03/15)	Award: 31 October 2011	An expropriation requires a substantial deprivation not only of the benefits, but the use of the investment; even an important loss of value is not sufficient, if it is unrelated to the interference with the use or control of the investment
Ronald S. Lauder v. The Czech Republic, UNCITRAL	Final Award, 3 September 2001	Expropriation requires an act initiated by the state and the act has to result in a benefit for the state
Malicorp v Egypt (ICSID Case No. ARB/08/18)	7 February 2011	The tribunal rejected the investor's claim of expropriation as the respondent was justified in terminating the contract, and this action could not be interpreted as an expropriatory measure.
Spyridon Roussalis v. Romania (ICSID Case No. ARB/06/1)	Award: 7 December 2011	To amount to expropriation a measure must constitute a deprivation of economic use and enjoyment, as if the related rights had ceased to exist. Omissions can constitute an expropriation. The state's intention and the purpose of the measure are relevant, but not decisive when determining whether an expropriation occurred.
Railroad Development Corporation v. Republic of Guatemala (ICSID Case No. ARB/07/23)	Award: 29 June 2012	No expropriation. The authorities on expropriation are numerous and largely depend on their own facts. A common theme is that an effect of the measures is that the claimant is deprived substantially of the use and benefits of the investment.

Annex 3

191

Case	Date	Summary
Edf v Argentina **(ICSID Case No ARB/03/23)**	Award: 11 June 2012	The tribunal rejected the claimant's claims for indirect expropriation
Ulysseas Inc. v Ecuador	12 June 2012	Opinion discusses discriminatory & arbitrary treatment, and "temporary" and indirect expropriation.
Renta 4 S.V.S.A., et al v. The Russian Federation **(SCC No. 24/2007)**	Award, 20 July 2012	Expropriation may arise from a series of actions which taken individually may not amount to such.
Electrabel S.A. v. Republic of Hungary **(ICSID Case No. ARB/07/19)**	Decision on Jurisdiction, Applicable Law and Liability, 30 November 2012	In order to prove indirect expropriation the claimant was required to prove that its investment had lost all significant economic value following the early termination of a power purchase agreement.
Burlington Resources Inc. v. Republic of Ecuador **(ICSID Case No. ARB/08/5)**	Decision on Liability: 14 December 2012	The Tribunal ruled that Ecuador unlawfully expropriated the company's significant oil investments. The Tribunal also found that Burlington's investment included the contractual right to be indemnified for the effects of Law 42, which, if enforced would materially have depleted its contractual position.
Inmaris Perestroika Sailing Maritime Services GmbH and Others v. Ukraine **(ICSID Case No ARB/08/8)**	Award: 1 May 2013	The State had breached its obligations under Article 4(2) of the BIT by expropriating the Claimant's investment without payment of compensation.
Vannessa Ventures Ltd. v. Bolivarian Republic of Venezuela **(ICSID Case No. ARB(AF)/04/6)**	Award, 16 January 2013	Contractual rights are capable of being expropriated. In order to amount to an expropriation under international law, it is necessary that the conduct of the State should go beyond that which an ordinary contracting party could adopt – "legitimate contractual responses" to contractual breaches will not suffice.

192

Case	Date	Summary
ConocoPhillips Petrozuata B.V., ConocoPhillips Hamaca B.V. and ConocoPhillips Gulf of Paria B.V. v. Bolivarian Republic of Venezuela (ICSID Case No. ARB/07/30)	Decision on Jurisdiction and Merits, 3 September 2013	While compensation for expropriation is not required at the moment of expropriation, parties must engage in good faith negotiations to fix the compensation in terms of the standard set if a payment satisfactory to the investor is not proposed at the outset.
Mr. Franck Charles Arif v. Republic of Moldova (ICSID Case No. ARB/11/23)	Award, 8 April 2013	Significant legal insecurity in respect of the claimant's investment could not amount to an expropriation of the claimant's investment where, for the moment, the claimant had not been deprived of the use and benefit of his investment (even where such deprivation appeared imminent).

6. MOST FAVOURED NATION

Case	Date	Summary
AES Summit Generation Limited and AES-Tisza Erömü Kft. v. Hungary (ICSID Case No ARB/07/22)	Award: 23 September 2010	The Tribunal found that Hungry did not breach its ECT obligation to provide Most Favoured trading status to AES.
Impregilo SpA v Argentina Republic (ICSID Case No ARB/07/17)	Award: 21 June 2011	The Tribunal held that the MFN clause in the Argentina-UK BIT did extend to the dispute resolution provisions and therefore did not exempt ICS from complying with the litigation prerequisite. (Contrast with ICS and Hochtief). MFN clauses can apply to dispute settlement provisions, at least if the MFN clause extends to "all matters regulated by the IIT".
Hochtief v Argentina (ICSID Case No ARB/07/31)	Award: 24 October 2011	Not every activity falls within the scope of an MFN clause. An MFN clause does not permit an investor to selectively pick provisions from several IITs; the investor has to rely on the whole scheme of one IIT, e.g. a dispute settlement clause. The Tribunal held that the MFN clause in the Argentina-UK BIT did extend to the dispute resolution provisions and therefore did not exempt ICS from complying with the litigation prerequisite. The opportunity to commence an arbitration without observing a waiting clause is not a distinct right; it concerns the exercise of an existing right to arbitrate and thus is within the scope of an MFN clause. (Contrast with Impreglio and ICS)

Case	Date	Summary
White Industries Australia Ltd v India UNCITRAL	Award: 30 November 2011	Tribunal did have jurisdiction over the dispute – the arbitration award at issue arose from a long-term contract between the parties, and was protected as a "continuation or transformation of the original investment". The MFN clause allowed Claimant to incorporate provision from the India/Kuwait BIT, and India was in breach of the obligation to provide "effective means" of resolving the claim.
ICS Inspection and Control Services Limited (United Kingdom) v. The Republic of Argentina (UNCITRAL, PCA Case No. 2010-9)	Award on Jurisdiction, 10 February 2012	Found that MFN clause of the Argentina-UK BIT did not apply in a way which would allow the claimant to make use of the dispute resolution provision in the Argentina-Lithuania BIT. In principle states are capable of drafting MFN clauses applicable to dispute settlement matters; if, however, the clause is not explicit in this regard, a tribunal must not use policy considerations (such as a tendency for treaty shopping) but an analysis of the IIT text to elaborate its meaning.

Case	Date	Summary
Daimler Financial Services AG v. Argentine Republic (ICSID Case No. ARB/05/1)	Award, 22 August 2012	The majority of the tribunal declined jurisdiction on the basis that the investor had failed to first submit the dispute to the Argentine courts for 18 months, as required by the Argentina-Germany BIT. The majority of the tribunal also held that the MFN clause did not extend to dispute resolution provisions, and therefore it did not enable investors to take advantage of arbitration clauses from Argentina's other bilateral investment treaties. If an MFN clause does not explicitly apply to "all matters subject to the IIT", this omission may constitute a supplementary indication that the state parties did not intend the MFN clause to cover dispute settlement provisions. If a state had intended for its IITs' MFN clause to apply to their international dispute resolution provisions, it would not have included a procedural requirement in the IIT that would instantly be rendered futile by the MFN clause.
Teinver S.A., Transportes de Cercanías S.A. and Autobuses Urbanos del Sur S.A. v. The Argentine Republic (ICSID CaseNo. ARB/09/1)	Decision on Jurisdiction, 21 December 2012	The Tribunal held that the claimants had satisfied the pre-conditions to arbitration contained in the Spain-Argentina BIT. The majority also held that, if those pre-conditions were not satisfied, the claimants could rely on the MFN clause in the BIT, to benefit from the dispute settlement provisions in the Australia-Argentina BIT, which did not contain those pre-conditions.
Garanti Koza LLP v. Turkmenistan (ICSID Case No. ARB/11/20)	Decision on Jurisdiction, 3 July 2013	"Most favoured nation" clauses are "a fiercely contested no-man's land in international law". Conflicting decisions are common (contrast, for example, Garanti Koza LLP v. Turkmenistan (ICSID Case No. ARB/11/20) with Kilic Insaat Ithalat Ihracat Sanayi ve Ticaret Anonim Sirketi v. Turkmenistan (ICSID Case No. ARB/10/1)).

7. UMBRELLA CLAUSE

Case	Date	Summary
Salini Costruttori S.p.A. and Italstrade S.p.A. v. The Hashemite Kingdom of Jordan, ICSID Case No. ARB/02/13	15 November 2004	Umbrella clauses have to be distinguished from other clauses, in particular clauses which merely commit the State to create a legal framework also apt to guarantee, inter alia, compliance with undertakings assumed with regard to specific investors.
Societe Generale de Surveillance SA v Paraguay **(ICSID Case No ARB/07/29)**	Award: 10 February 2012	The tribunal found that the respondent was in breach of the umbrella clause. A contractual obligation is a commitment within the meaning of an umbrella clause. An exclusive jurisdiction clause in a contract does not bar a tribunal from examining a contract breach as a breach of an umbrella clause. An umbrella clause cannot only be breached by actions that a commercial counterparty cannot take; i.e., an abuse of state power is not required. Without any textual limitations, an umbrella clause may apply to all kind of commitments by a state.
Bosh International, Inc and B&P Ltd Foreign Investments Enterprise v. Ukraine **(ICSID Case No. ARB/08/11)**	Award on Jurisdiction and Liability: 25 October 2012	Found that for the respondent university's claim to be attributable to the Ukraine for the purposes of the relevant BIT and it umbrella clause, it would have to be empowered by law to exercise elements of government authority, and that its conduct would have to be related to the exercise of that authority. In this case second limb not made out.
Micula et al v. Romania (ICSID Case No. ARB/05/20)	Award, 11 December 2013	Depending on the language used in the BIT, the umbrella clause may cover obligations of any nature, regardless of their source (both contractual and non-contractual obligations).

8. DENIAL OF JUSTICE

Case	Date	Summary
Liman Caspian Oil B.V. and NCL Dutch Investment B.V. v. Kazakhstan	Award, 22 June 2010	The fair and equitable treatment standard under the Energy Charter Treaty was not limited to the minimum standard under customary international law, and the prohibition of denial of justice formed part of the fair and equitable treatment standard. It was possible that the actions of state courts may breach the fair and equitable treatment standard even if they do not amount to denial of justice.
White Industries Australia Ltd v India UNCITRAL	Award: 30 November 2011	The Tribunal found that Claimant did not show that there was a denial of justice or expropriation.
Philip Morris Brand Sàrl (Switzerland), Philip Morris Products S.A. (Switzerland) and Abal Hermanos S.A. (Uruguay) v. Oriental Republic of Uruguay (ICSID Case No. ARB/10/7)	Decision on Jurisdiction: 2 July 2013	Tribunal had jurisdiction under Article 46 of the ICSID Convention over the Claimants' claim for denial of justice
Dan Cake (Portugal) S.A. v Hungary (ICSID Case No. ARB/12/9)	Decision on Jurisdiction and Liability, 24 August 2015	A decision of the Hungarian bankruptcy court (which, it was not disputed, was under international law attributable to the State itself) was a violation of the obligation to treat the investor in a fair and equitable manner which took the form of a denial of justice.

9. QUANTIFICATION

Case	Date	Summary
Lemire v Ukraine (**ICSID Case No ARB/06/18**)	Award: 28 March 2011	Discusses quantification of damages for breach of the obligation for fair and equitable treatment, and the availability of moral damages.
Edf v Argentina (**ICSID Case No ARB/03/23**)	Award: 11 June 2012	Reasserted the duty of claimants to take reasonable steps to mitigate damage.
Quasar de Valors SICAV S.A., and Others v. The Russian Federation, (**SCC No. 24/2007**)	Award: 20 July 2012	The tribunal found that the claimant's interest were expropriated and discussed the value of compensation to be given.
Rompetrol Group N.V. v. Romania (*ICSID Case No. ARB/06/3*)	Award, 6 May 2013	Although there had been a breach of the "fair and equitable treatment standard", no damages would be award due to the claimant's failure to demonstrate any loss stemming from that breach. The application of the "event study method" (which is an empirical technique used to measure the stock price impact of a specific event, such as a company's earnings announcement) was inherently questionable – a more appropriate method would be one which allowed for an objective comparison between the status quo and the claimant's position at the time the claim was commenced. Tribunals should adopt a considerable degree of caution in awarding "moral" damages to a corporate investor, and discretionary moral damages should not be awarded solely on the grounds of an inability to prove actual economic loss.
Gold Reserve Inc. v. Bolivarian Republic of Venezuela (ICSID Case No. ARB(AF)/09/1)	Award, 22 September 2014	Tribunal held that the number, variety and seriousness of the breaches made the FET violation by Venezuela particularly egregious, and the compensation due to Gold Reserve for such breaches had to reflect the seriousness of the violation.

Annex 3

Case	Date	Summary
Tidewater Investment SRL and Tidewater Caribe, C.A. v. Bolivarian Republic of Venezuela (ICSID Case No. ARB/10/5)	Award (March 13, 2015	Tribunal (having found that the expropriation was lawful) considered the relevance and application of the compensation standard in the determination of the lawfulness of the expropriation. In the view of the Tribunal, an expropriation wanting only a determination of compensation by an international tribunal was not to be treated as an illegal expropriation.
		Tribunal endorsed the World Bank Guidelines as providing reasonable guidance as to the content of the standard chosen by the States Parties to the BIT as the standard of compensation to be applied in cases of lawful compensation, where the investment constituted a going concern at the time of the taking. Absent agreement of the parties, the Guidelines define the fair market value as to be determined 'according to reasonable criteria related to the market value of the investment, i.e., in an amount that a willing buyer would normally pay to a willing seller after taking into account the nature of the investment, the circumstances in which it would operate in the future and its specific characteristics, including the period in which it has been in existence, the proportion of tangible assets in the total investment and other relevant factors pertinent to the specific circumstances of each case'.
		Tribunal noted that while the compensation in a lawful expropriation was to be considered as at immediately before the expropriation, this does not mean that the valuation would be unconcerned with future prospects: (1) as the World Bank Guidelines themselves confirm, the factors that a willing buyer would itself take into account on the purchase of such an investment necessarily include 'the circumstances in which it would operate in the future'; and (2) the Tribunal is not required to shut its eyes to events subsequent to the date of injury, if these shed light in more concrete terms on the value applicable at the date of injury or validate the reasonableness of a valuation made at that date.